Thomas Cook

HOTSPOTS
DOMINICAN
REPUBLIC

CW00621258

Written by Lura Seavey
Front cover photography courtesy of Thomas Cook Tour Operations Ltd

Original design concept by Studio 183 Limited
Series design by the Bridgewater Book Company
Cover design/artwork by Lee Biggadike, Studio 183 Limited

Produced by the Bridgewater Book Company
The Old Candlemakers, West Street, Lewes, East Sussex BN7 2NZ, United Kingdom
www.bridgewaterbooks.co.uk
Project Editor: Emily Casey Bailey
Project Designer: Lisa McCormick

Published by Thomas Cook Publishing
A division of Thomas Cook Tour Operations Limited
PO Box 227, Units 15-16, Coningsby Road, Peterborough PE3 8SB, United Kingdom
email: books@thomascook.com
www.thomascookpublishing.com
+ 44 (0) 1733 416477

ISBN-13: 978-1-84157-564-3
ISBN-10: 1-84157-564-X

First edition © 2006 Thomas Cook Publishing
Text © 2006 Thomas Cook Publishing
Maps © 2006 Thomas Cook Publishing
Project Editor: Diane Ashmore
Production/DTP Editor: Steven Collins

Printed and bound in Spain by Graficas Cems, Navarra, Spain

CONTENTS

SYMBOLS KEY

The following is a key to the symbols used throughout this book:

i information office	**✝** church	**¶¶** restaurant
🚌 bus stop	**✈** airport	**▣** café
✚ hospital	**↘** tip	**Ⴤ** bar
✉ post office	**🛍** shopping	**◉** fine dining

---

① telephone   **f** fax   **e** email   **W** website address

a address   **◷** opening times   **❶** important

€ budget price   €€ mid-range price   €€€ most expensive

★ specialist interest   ★★ see if passing   ★★★ top attraction

---

INTRODUCTION
Getting to know the Dominican Republic

ATLANTIC OCEAN

N

| 0 | 20 km | 40 km |
| 0 | 10 miles | 20 miles |

NAGUA

Bahía de Escoceso

Samaná Peninsula

SAMANÁ

Bahía de Samaná'

Parqué Nacional los Haitises

SABANA DE LA MER

MONTE PLATA

Cordillera Oriental

HATO MAYOR

EL SEIBO

Playa Bavaro

HIGÜEY

PUNTA CAÑA

SANTO DOMINGO

Parqué Nacional Submarino la Caleta

BOCA CHICA

SAN PEDRO DE MACORIS

LA ROMANA

Isla Catalina

Parqué Nacional del Este

Isla Saona

UNITED STATES OF AMERICA

Atlantic Ocean

Gulf of Mexico

DOMINICAN REPUBLIC

CUBA

HAITI

MEXICO

JAMAICA

Caribbean Sea

GUATEMALA

HONDURAS

NICARAGUA

Pacific Ocean

VENEZUELA

Getting to know the Dominican Republic

Jagged mountains peek up between the Caribbean and the Atlantic, surveying the sandy shores and clear blue waters. The sound of music in the distance beckons the visitor closer, while the fresh evening breeze after siesta refreshes and invigorates the once-weary traveller.

GEOGRAPHY

Occupying two-thirds of the island of Hispañiola, the Dominican Republic covers an area of 48,734 sq km (18, 816 sq miles). The western third of the island is occupied by Haiti, and the Haitian border region is the least developed, and least travelled, area of the Dominican Republic. Haiti itself has had periods of instability in the past, and it is wise to check with the Foreign Office before considering a trip over this border.

Because of the island's formation as a chain of mountains jutting out of the sea, the development of the country has been determined by the landscape. Pico Duarte, which sits in the western region of the country in the Cordillera Central mountain chain, is the island's tallest peak, reaching 3087 m (10,128 ft). The Cordillera Septentrional is a ridge of lower mountains which defines the northwestern coast, while the Cordillera Oriental forms the eastern end of the island.

Naturally, with all of these mountains come plentiful valleys and the streams and rivers that accompany them – the longest river is the Yaque del Norte, extending 296 km (184 miles) long. The Cibao Valley, which is in the basin of the Yaque del Norte, reaps the benefits of the constant feed from the mountains and is known as a fertile region for grain and tobacco farming. A good portion of the Dominican landscape is covered in lush greenery, boasting over 5600 species of plants. But there are also stark contrasts: you could visit a rainforest and its giant trees one day, and on the next, see cacti in the desert. Among native plants are the cashew, coconut, guava and star fruit, as well as the much-coveted mahogany and ebony trees.

● *Palm tree overlooks Bavaro beach in Punta Caña*

LIFESTYLE

Modern Dominicans unfortunately cannot afford the same luxuries as visitors. Traditional industries based on crops such as sugar cane, which used to employ many workers, have given way to less expensive alternatives like corn syrup, rendering jobs redundant. Although tourism has brought in other jobs, most hotels are foreign-owned and operated, offering only entry-level positions to locals. For most who live and work on the island, the realities of frequent electrical blackouts and freshwater shortages are a daily problem. However, despite the enormous socio-economic gap, Dominicans are known to be friendly, welcoming hosts.

HISTORY

The Dominican Republic was originally the stronghold of the Taino Indians until the arrival of Columbus in 1492. He named the island Hispañiola ('Little Spain') and returned with a thousand colonists the following year. The original settlement, La Isabela (see page 63), was abandoned after just a few years and shifted to the present site of Santo Domingo. After numerous pirate attacks, Spain finally ceded the western third of the island to France in 1697. Years of fighting followed until this became the republic of Haiti in 1804. In 1821, the Dominican Republic was formed, although full independence from Spain was not achieved until 1865. In the 1930s, the country was in the grip of the right-wing dictator Rafael Trujillo until his assassination in 1961, when Joaquin Balaguer came to power.

TRADITIONS & RELIGION

Although many aspects of Dominican life have changed in the past few decades, some stand strong as always. Baseball, for one, will always be a strong national pastime. You will find that most towns have a team, and if a game is being played, not much else will be happening! Religion is also important; most Dominicans are Roman Catholic, although there is an underlying influence of old voodoo on the island.

 Visitors are often welcomed with a smile by the locals

The best of the Dominican Republic

WHALE WATCHING IN SAMANÁ
Each year during the humpback whale migration and mating season in February and March, whales can be viewed in astounding numbers off the shores of the Samaná peninsula (see page 43) and even the rare baby whales can be seen.

HISTORICAL SANTO DOMINGO
The first city of the New World, Santo Domingo (see pages 14–23) is filled with a large number of thrilling historical sites. Visitors can see the country's first church and hospital, plus museums housing ancient Taino artefacts.

CABARETE – THE WINDSURFING CAPITAL
Home to one of the best beaches for this sport, Cabarete's beach (see pages 49–50) provides just the right winds to facilitate windsurfing nearly every day. Kiteboarding is picking up speed here too, and the town is host to international competitions for both.

BOCA CHICA – THE ALL-TIME PARTY
If letting your hair down is what your idea of a holiday is about, then the town of Boca Chica (see page 24) is for you. The rum is flowing and the merengue is playing loud, so come and have some fun!

DIVING IN SOSÚA
A diver's paradise, Sosúa (see page 53) has dozens of amazing sites suited to adventurers at all skill levels. Explore the magnificent reefs, swim with bright tropical fish and relax in some of the most picturesque surroundings on the island!

RESORTS
Places under the sun

Santo Domingo
first city of the New World

At the top of the list in this exciting city is the area known as the Zona Colonial, where you can find many of the 'firsts' of the New World still intact, as well as others in ruins. From the Parque Independencia, where Juan Pablo Duarte and his fellow revolutionaries led the country to freedom against the Haitians, to the Alcazar de Colón, this part of the town is rich in history, beginning with the earliest European settlers. After you have explored the old town, there's plenty more – modern Santo Domingo has a multitude of great shops, fantastic restaurants and outstanding nightlife.

When visiting the capital, it is hard to miss the five-mile oceanfront stretch known as the **Malecón**. The official street name is Avenida George Washington, and it is lined with an abundance of clubs, hotels, restaurants, bars, and various other places to rest and have a drink. It is especially popular with younger visitors, and often the festivities do not begin here until very late in the evening, continuing into the early morning hours. If this is too late for you, don't be alarmed – there is plenty of shopping and food to be found along the main strip of the Zona Colonial during regular touring times throughout the day.

The **Calle el Conde** in the Zona Colonial is as fast-paced and busy as you would expect a main city street to be, and you will find as many modern conveniences here as you would need. Automated Teller Machines (ATMs/cash machines) and even some fast food chains have moved into the area because of its popularity, and souvenir shops accept credit cards.

There is a tourist office on Isabela la Católica in the Zona Colonial, but English is rarely spoken here. You are advised to ask your concierge or host for information rather than depending on government-run information offices.

THINGS TO SEE & DO (GREATER SANTO DOMINGO)
Acuario Nacional (National Aquarium) ★ ★ ★
Visitors can experience underwater life in a unique way here as they
walk through a plexiglass tunnel while sharks and fish swim all around.
Tamaury the manatee greets visitors from a pool, while shallow areas
are open for children and adults to meet friendly sea creatures such as
turtles. ➋ Avenida España ➊ 809 592 1509 ➍ Open Tues–Sun
09.00–17.30, closed Mon ➊ Admission charge

Agua Splash ★ ★
Especially popular with the children, this typical water park with waterslides and pools is a cooling diversion on a hot day. Weekends can be very
crowded with tourists and local families. ➋ Avenida España ➊ 809 591
5927 ➍ Open Tues–Sun 10.30–17.00, closed Mon ➊ Admission charge

Cuevas De Los Tres Ojos (Caves of the Three Eyes) ★ ★
Each cave is entered by a lake, clear and bright blue. One site requires the
use of a ferry (at additional charge), and some walking on steep rocky
steps is required so take care to wear proper footwear. Set on the east
bank of the Ozama River, this jungle-type atmosphere has been the site
for many film shoots. The site was also once a very spiritual place for the
natives of the island. ➋ Avenida Las Americas ➊ No telephone
➍ Open daily 09.30–17.30 ➊ Admission charge

Faro a Colón (Columbus Lighthouse) ★
Although this has been quite a controversial structure in many ways due
to its cost, placement and other problems, it can be stunning when lit
and is certainly a landmark of Dominican history. Shaped like a giant
cross, the lighthouse was the inflated idea of Joaquin Balaguer during
his regime as leader since the 1960s. Although many other places
claim the same, the remains of Columbus are supposedly within the
walls. ➋ Parque Mirador del Este ➊ 809 592 1492 ➍ Open daily
09.30–17.30 ➊ Admission charge

PADRE CASTELLANOS

Río Ozama

AVENIDA MAXIMO GOMEZ

AVENIDA DUARTE

AVENIDA VENEZUELA

6

AVENIDA 27 DE FEBRERO

AVENIDA LAS AMÉRICAS

**CUEVAS DE
LOS TRES OJOS**

BOCA CHICA

IDA JOHN KENNEDY

limpico
Pablo
rte

**Parque
Mirador
del Este**

FARO A COLÓN ●

**ZONA
COLONIAL**
See
map on
page 20

Plaza de
La Cultura

AVENIDA 30 DE MARZO

● **PARQUE
INDEPENDENCIA**

**ACUARIO NACIONAL
AGUA SPLASH** →

ue

AVENIDA BOLÍVAR

AVENIDA ESPAÑA

AVENIDA INDEPENDENCIA

MALECÓN (AVENIDA GEORGE WASHINGTON)

NTRAL SANTO DOMINGO
See map on page 19

CARIBBEAN
SEA

N

Jardín Botánico Nacional (Botanical Gardens) ★★★

Santo Domingo's botanical garden is the largest in the Caribbean. The extensive grounds can be viewed from a small train (passage included in admission), or you may walk the gardens by yourself or with a guide. The Japanese garden is a favourite attraction, with a lovely pagoda for shade, and the 300 varieties of orchids found in the remainder of the garden are astounding. The site also attracts many species of birds and other wildlife. ⓐ Avenida Jardin and Avenida de los Proceres ☎ 809 565 2860 ⌚ Open Tues–Sun 09.00–17.00, closed Mon ⓘ Admission charge

Parque Zoológico Nacional (National Zoo) ★★★

A visit to the zoo offers the opportunity to view a strange assortment of creatures up close, such as crocodiles, hyenas and flamingos. The rarest of animals that lives at this zoo is Hispañiola's native solenodon, a small, anteater-like rodent that is near extinction and exists nowhere else in the world. ⓐ Paseo de los Reyes Catolicos and Avenida Jose Ortega y Gassett ☎ 809 563 3149 ⌚ Open Mon–Fri 09.00–17.00, Sat–Sun 09.00–17.30 ⓘ Admission charge

THINGS TO SEE & DO (CENTRAL SANTO DOMINGO)

Plaza de la Cultura (The Cultural Plaza) is a complete city block set aside for four museums and a theatre, as detailed in the following entries. ⓐ Avenida Máximo Gómez and Avenida Dr Pedro Henriquez Ureña

> Visitors should be aware that they must be dressed appropriately in order to get into any of these museums – no beachwear, shorts, sleeveless shirts or otherwise inappropriate clothing is permitted.

Galeria de Arte Moderno (Modern Art Museum) ★★

Set up to give this century's Dominican artists more prominence, many visitors will be surprised at the wide subject range of this museum. ☎ 809 685 2153 ⌚ Open Tues–Sun 10.00–17.00, closed Mon ⓘ Admission charge

CENTRAL SANTO DOMINGO

AVENIDA MÉXICO

AVENIDA MÁXIMO GÓMEZ

AVENIDA DR PEDRO HGUEZ UREÑA

LEOPOLDO NAVARRO

AVENIDA BOLÍVAR

Plaza de la Cultura

que

AVENIDA BOLÍVAR

JOSÉ CONTRERAS

CALLE SANTIAGO

CALLE SOCORRO SÁNCHEZ

CASIMIRO N. DE MOYA

JUAN SÁNCHEZ RAMÍREZ

UNIVERSIDAD AUTÓNOMA DE SANTO DOMINGO

PALACIO DE BELLAS ARTES

AVENIDA INDEPENDENCIA

MALECÓN (AVENIDA GEORGE WASHINGTON)

CALLE BENIGNO F. ROJAS

CALLE DR PIÑEYRO

CARIBBEAN SEA

N

0   1 km

0   0.5 miles

1. GALERÍA DE ARTE MODERNO
2. MUSEO DE HISTORIA Y GEOGRAFÍA
3. MUSEO DE HISTORIA NATURAL
4. MUSEO DEL HOMBRE DOMINICANO
5. TEATRO NACIONAL

Museo de Historia Natural (Natural History Museum) ★★

This museum offers a planetarium with a laser presentation about the galaxy. There are many exhibits that focus on the geology of the country, such as fossils and larimar (a blue gem of volcanic origin, found only in the Dominican Republic), and there is a large section explaining exactly what amber is composed of, as well as how it is formed. Other attractions include a huge whale skeleton and many of the island's native animals on display, stuffed. This is a popular museum with children.

Rio Ozam

AVENIDA MEXICO

BENITO GONZÁLEZ

JACINTO DE LA CONCHA

AVENIDA MELLA

JOSE REYES

JUAN ISIDRO PÉREZ

ALTAGRACIA

COLON

LA ATARAZANA

RESTAURACIÓN

EMILIANO TEJERA

ALCÁZAR DE COLÓN

Plaza de España

ISABELLA LA CATOLICA

3

JUAN ISIDRO PÉREZ

Parque

SANTOMÉ

SANTIAGO RODRIGUEZ

RUINAS DE LA HOSPITAL DE SAN NICOLAS DE BARI

CALLE GENERAL LUPERÓN

LAS MERCEDES

SALOMÉ UREÑA

CASA FRANCIA

MUSEO MUNDO DE AMBAR

ARZOBISPO MERIÑO

CALLE DE LAS DAMAS

AVENIDA DA

Parque colon

1

CALLE HOSTOS

CALLE EL CONDE (PEDESTRIAN)

AVENIDA DUARTE

JOSE REYES

CATEDRAL DE LAS AMÉRICAS

SANTOMÉ

Parque Independencia

ARZOBISPO NOUEL

PADRE BILLINI

ARZOBISPO PORTES

PALO MINCADO

PASEO PRESIDENTE BILLINI

N

ZONA COLONIAL

0   10
0   300

☎ 809 689 0106 ⏰ Open Tues–Sun 10.00–17.00, closed Mon
ℹ Admission charge

Museo de Historia y Geografia (History and Geography Museum) ★

Here, history aficionados can see relics of past dictator Trujillo, including a car from his motorcade (filled with bullets) from the day he was assassinated, or stop by the electric chair once used for torture. ☎ 809 686 6668 ⏰ Open Tues–Sun 09.30–17.00, closed Mon ℹ Admission charge

Museo del Hombre Dominicano (Museum of Dominican Man) ★

You need to bypass the first two floors to find the collections in this museum. Here you will see an extensive collection of Taino artefacts including jewellery, weapons, and artwork, such as sculptures of gods. Other collections include a display on the slave trade and its impact on the country. A separate exhibit emphasizes in detail how the mixture of cultures have affected Catholicism and religion in the country. A popular exhibit is the model *campesino* house, whch shows in great detail the simplicity of Dominican rural life outside the cities. ☎ 809 687 3623 ⏰ Open Tues–Sun 10.00–17.00, closed Mon ℹ Admission charge

Teatro Nacional (National Theatre) ★

This theatre holds performances and other events. ☎ 809 687 3191 ⏰ Open Tues–Sun, by schedule

THINGS TO SEE & DO (ZONA COLONIAL)
Alcázar de Colón (The Palace of Colombus) ★★

This palace has been fully restored to its former glory after once becoming nearly a pile of rubble. During its initial construction in 1510, not even one nail was used. It was the home of Diego Colón (Columbus' eldest son) and his family, and was the country's prominent palace until their departure some six decades later. ⓐ Plaza de España ☎ 809 685 9072 ⏰ Open daily 09.00–17.00 ℹ Admission charge

Casa Francia (French House) ★

Fascinating less for the actual structure and more for its pedigree, this building is now home to the French Embassy. Among its past dwellers are Diego Velazquez, Hernán Cortés and Francisco Pizarro. ❸ Calle de las Damas and Calle El Conde ⏱ Embassy open Mon–Fri 09.00–16.30, closed Sat and Sun ❶ No admission to the public

Ruinas de la Hospital de San Nicolás de Bari
(Ruins of the St. Nicholas of Bari Hospital) ★

This site was the first hospital built by the European settlers in the New World. ❸ Calle Hostos and Calle General Luperón ☎ No telephone ❶ No admission charge

CARNIVAL!

Each year, residents of Santo Domingo combine their traditional pre-Lenten festivities in February with their **Independence Day holiday**, making the entire month one celebration, all culminating on 27 February to re-create the revolution in 1844 at the Parque Independencia.

Celebrated every Sunday in February and ending in a huge event at the end of the month right before Lent, Carnival is filled with parades, parties, dancing and fun for all.

Santo Domingo holds one of the most boisterous and well-known celebrations, drawing in crowds from all over the world. Residents spend the entire year working on their artistic and flamboyant costumes. Masks depicting *el Diablo* (the devil) are very common, as well as bright and festive dresses.

The city also hosts several other festivals throughout the year, including the **Latin Music Festival** in June, the **Merengue Festival** in July and August, and the **Restoration Festival** in August (see Festivals & events, page 108).

Museo Mundo de Ambar (Amber World Museum) ★
Displays and a workshop (see page 90). ⓐ Arzobispo Merino 452 ⓣ 809
682 3309 ⓦ www.amberworldmuseum.com ⓛ Open daily 09.00–18.00

RESTAURANTS (see maps on pages 16–17, 19 and 20)

Alfatori Restaurant €€–€€€ ❶ (see page 20) International
dishes served in an upmarket environment. Live music is also
often a feature. ⓐ Arzobispo Meriño 115, next to the Catedral de las
Américas (First Church of America) ⓣ 809 221 2109 ⓦ www.alfatori.com

Mesón de la Cava €€ ❷ (see pages 16–17) Fine international
cuisine, along with lovely atmosphere. ⓐ Avenida Mirador del
Sur 1 ⓣ 809 533 2818

Pasatiempo Ristorante Pizzería Italiana € ❸ (see page 20)
Fantastic pizzas, calzones and other traditional Italian specialities
available here. ⓐ Isabel la Católica 204 ⓣ 809 689 4823

Restaurant Vesuvio Tiradentes €€ ❹ (see page 19) Italian fare
in a pleasant setting. ⓐ Avenida Tiradentes 17 ⓣ 809 562 6060
ⓦ www.vesuviotiradentes.com

NIGHTLIFE

The five mile stretch of beachfront known as the **Malecón** (see pages
16–17) is a collection of nightclubs, bars, restaurants and assorted shops
to fit just about anyone's taste. ⓐ Avenida George Washington ⓛ Lively
late at night until early morning hours

Discoteca Jubilee ❺ (see page 19) A place to dance the night away.
ⓐ Renaissance Jaragua Night Club and Casino, Calle de los Héroes 29
ⓣ 809 533 2151 ⓛ Open daily, 24 hours

Eclipse ❻ (see pages 16–17) Popular with younger, local crowds. Plays
current international hits. ⓐ Avenida Venezuela 64 ⓣ 809 593 3336

Boca Chica
party-town of the Caribbean

Still a lovely spot, this once-coveted location has, in recent years, earned a reputation for being host to one constant party. The city has a lively and carefree atmosphere and there is always the sound of very loud music playing somewhere. Yet the water is still a radiant blue and there is plenty of fun to be had for everyone.

Weekends here are especially crowded, when people who live in Santo Domingo make the short 25 km (16 mile) trip to swim at the perfect beach. The shallow waters here are the biggest attraction, extending at wading height far enough to walk to an island.

Boca Chica has not always been the wild-child offshoot of the capital city. As a resort town, it was once quite exclusive and the holiday favourite for wealthy visitors from abroad. Long before that, the native Taino appreciated the area's natural beauty as well; after an extensive archaeological dig, this same spot was found to have been a major Taino centre.

If you want to join in on the seaside merengue and rum, remember that day time is far safer than the night time for travellers here. Tourists of both sexes are likely to be approached by prostitutes and drug dealers in all parts of the city when joining in festivities after dark.

THINGS TO SEE & DO
Playa Boca Chica ★★★
The beach is divided roughly into three sections, with the eastern section restricted to those staying at a beachfront resort. The central section of the beach is the most lively party-zone, and can be accessed at the end

---

▶ *Playa Boca Chica has plenty of amenities for everyone*

◉ Divers can explore a sunken ship and the surrounding coral reef

of Calle Hungria. You will find most anything you need beachside here, including food, drink, and light shopping. The western end of the beach is quieter and usually more suitable for families. The food found here is served in local-type shacks.

EXCURSION
Parque Nacional Submarino la Caleta ★
Now a coral-reef in the making, the main attraction at this national park is the scuttled treasure hunt ship, *The Hickory*. At its deepest, the protected area reaches 180 m (590 ft), making it highly accessible to divers who want to explore the open hull and tropical undersea life. The park also includes a small museum of Taino artefacts. There is no official diving service set up, so making prior arrangements with your guide is highly recommended, rather than choosing one of the many fishermen who are looking to make extra money. ⓐ Route 66, 22 km (14 miles) east of Santo Domingo

RESTAURANTS
You will not be hard pressed to find either fast food or traditional Dominican fare virtually anywhere along the beach and in the tourist areas of the city.

La Criolla € Highly recommended for traditional Dominican food. Often busy, even in the wee hours of the morning.
ⓐ Calle Duarte ⓣ No telephone ⓛ Open daily, 24 hours

Neptuno's €€ Known for its extraordinary fresh seafood, it is best to hire a taxicab to bring you to this restaurant.
ⓐ Calle Duarte 12 ⓣ 809 523 4703 ⓛ Open daily for brunch and dinner
ⓘ Reservations recommended

San Pedro de Macoris
where stars are born

If you didn't know any better, this old sugar cane area might seem somewhat run-down. In fact it is home to several of the world's most productive Major League Baseball training camps and has produced many incredible athletes. Despite the economic struggles that San Pedro has faced after losing the sugar cane industry and being hit by ruthless hurricanes, *beisbol* (baseball) still keeps spirits high.

The high poverty and homelessness rate in San Pedro may deter some from visiting, but the people are determined and make the best of their home. There is more than just baseball for the residents to be proud of. Here you will find a wider range of cultural backgrounds than in many other places, and as a result the festivals and parades have their own certain spice. The architecture has a heavy Victorian influence due to the timing of the city's greatest wealth gained from sugar.

PLAY BALL!

Baseball aficionados won't want to miss San Pedro, and should look into booking from late November to February in order to catch the training season. Major League teams from North America and Japanese teams have their own training grounds, and also use the local team's stadium for practice. It was this very city that raised the baseball stars Sammy Sosa, Tony Fernandez and Alfonso Soriano.

Recruiters from all the major teams also make this their home base, and as a result this is a central place for games to be played so that local talent can strut its stuff. It is considered certain success for a young man to attain a minor league contract, so many boys are groomed towards that goal from an early age.

⬥ *Baseball is more than just a popular pastime in San Pedro*

THINGS TO SEE & DO
Estadio Tetelo Vargas (Tetelo Vargas Stadium) ★ ★ ★
This ball field is the pride and joy of San Pedro's home team, Las Estrellas Orientals (the Eastern Stars). It is not uncommon to find Major League players working out here during the day, and the scouts are always hanging around looking for the next local superstar. Schedules for games can be found in newspapers as far away as Santo Domingo.

Games are usually played in the evening. ⓐ Avenida Circunvalación and Carretera Mella

George Bell Mansion ★
Baseball fans will want to stop by this huge monument to one of the city's first great Major League baseball heroes, built for him after he made his fame in the United States. ❸ Avenida 27 de Febrero

Iglesia San Pedro Apostol ★
This church is simple yet elegant in appearance, with a whitewashed exterior, three rows of pews and a mahogany altar. It was built in 1911 and the bell tower that rises so close to the shoreline has somehow survived even Hurricane Georges in 1998. ⓐ Avenida Charro and Independencia

Malecón ★★★
Although not anything like the Malecón of Santo Domingo, this is still a lively place where visitors are guaranteed to find plenty of local food shacks, vendors and activity. The views are beautiful, but swimming here is not such a good idea – pollution left from the city's industrial days is still an issue. ❸ Avenida Gaston F Deligne (which begins at Howard Johnson Hotel Macorìx)

RESTAURANTS
Much like other towns, there are often plenty of street vendors offering traditional foods wherever people congregate, especially along the beach. If you are looking for upper-scale cuisine, your best bet is to eat at your hotel.

Casa La Esquina Caliente € One of the only pizza places in town that isn't a foreign-owned chain. ⓐ Avenida Circunvalación 1 ❶ 809 529 0120

Pica Pollo La Ceniza € Fried chicken is the speciality here. ⓐ Calle F A Caamaño 40 ❶ 809 246 4038 ◐ Open daily from noon

Pittsburgh Pirates € Baseball-themed American-fare restaurant. ⓐ Calle Rufino Linares ⓕ 809 246 5712

 Mi Sitio € Casual, home-style atmosphere. ⓐ Avenida Malecón ⓕ 809 529 8373 ⓒ Open Tues–Sun for lunch and dinner

 El Taquito € Traditional Dominican, fast-food fare. ⓐ Calle Sánchez 20 ⓕ 809 529 2253 ⓒ Open daily, until late evening

NIGHTLIFE
Exótica Bar Café Typical, small nightclub atmosphere. ⓐ Calle R Mota ⓕ 809 529 9392

Restaurant Disco Terraza El Catedrático A restaurant that features music and dancing. ⓐ Avenida Circunvalación 20-A ⓕ 809 529 6887

ⓞ *Hotels usually offer diners a wide range of fresh seafood*

La Romana
the city that shines

La Romana is perhaps one of the country's most exclusive areas, made famous as the site of Lisa Marie Presley and Michael Jackson's wedding. Once a town made wealthy by the sugar cane industry, its main source of revenue is now tourism. The city is renowned for attracting celebrities from around the world, many of whom own private villas nearby.

⬤ *Relax at the luxurious Casa de Campo resort*

Exclusivity and very tight security are to be expected here, since a large section of the town is owned by the **Casa de Campo** resort. Guests there wear bracelets that act as their pass within the resort – which is so big they are advised to use a car just to get around the grounds.

The **Parque Central (Central Park)** in La Romana is a lovely place to visit to see some nice homes in the bright and festive colours that have become a trademark in the country. Here you will also find the parish church and the town hall, where visitors are welcome to stop in and say 'hola'! In the evening you will find fewer tourists and more local residents relaxing in the park, taking in the atmosphere and meeting friends. One block north you will find the **Mercado Modelo**, where prices on local arts and crafts may be slightly lower than in the other shops in town.

THINGS TO SEE & DO

Altos de Chavon ★★★

Often considered a shopping complex, this high-end tourist haven contains enough to occupy a visitor for at least an entire day. The decor is not quite Caribbean – it has an old-fashioned, slightly contrived, European look, perhaps the result of too much stucco and artificial ageing techniques. However, in addition to a wide range of shops, you will find plenty of good restaurants and evening entertainment.

Amphitheatre ★★

If you love music, you will want to find out about the shows being offered in the 5000-seat amphitheatre, including the annual Jazz Festival. This open-air stadium has been host to both modern and classic greats such as Shakira, Julio Iglesias, Frank Sinatra, Carlos Santana and many more. ❶ Contact your host or a local hotel for listings

Casa de Campo ★★

Non-guests are allowed to visit this resort, but arrangements should be made first if you are interested in using any of the facilities. Casa de Campo offers horseback riding, diving, entertainment, and a full array of outdoor activities. Three 18-hole golf courses and a skeet (clay pigeon) shooting course are open to the public with no prior arrangement needed. ☎ 305 856 7083 Ⓦ www.casadecampo.com.do

Church of St. Stanislaus ★★

Because if its popularity, this grand edifice is not as peaceful a retreat as one might hope, but it is well worth a stop to enjoy the architecture and views. The church's pride is the fountain of the four lions. ⓐ Main Plaza ⏰ Mass, Sat and Sun, 17.00; open when Mass not taking place

Rancho Cumayasa Eco ★★★

This resort offers non-staying guests the option of buying day passes, which include lunch, a one-hour horseback ride, access to paddleboats and admission to the resort's popular children's attraction 'Hurricane House'. ⓐ Highway 4 ☎ 809 757 0535 ❶ Admission charge

Regional Museum of Archaeology ★

This simple museum displays Taino artefacts and is a welcome break from the surrounding bustle. Exhibits are mainly from the personal collections of the archaeologist Samuel Pion. ⓐ Altos de Chavon ☎ 809 523 8554 ⏰ Open daily 09.00–20.00 ❶ No admission charge

RESTAURANTS

Giacosa Restaurante €€€ A stunning, rustic setting, with live piano music, a full bar and a patio overlooking the Chavón River. Full international wine selection suits the tasty, sophisticated Italian menu. ⓐ Altos de Chavon ☎ 809 523 8466 Ⓦ www.giacosa.com.do ⏰ Open daily from 11.00

Pica Pollo La Esperanza € Traditional, Dominican fried chicken. ⓐ H P Quezada 132 ☎ 809 556 3841

Pizzería Alondra € Privately owned and great for a quick bite. ⓐ F del C Márquez 88 ☎ 809 550 4115 ⏰ Open daily 11.00–23.00

SHOPPING

La Tienda Literally meaning 'the store', this is an upscale handicraft boutique. Much of the wares (such as the authentic Taino stationery) are tailored to the tastes and needs of American and European visitors, but it is an excellent gift shop when looking for something with a less rustic appearance. ⓐ Altos de Chavon ❶ 809 523 3333, ext. 5398 ⓛ Open daily 09.00–20.00

The Principal Gallery, the Rincón Gallery and the Loggia Gallery These three gallery spaces are connected, and each offers the chance to view contemporary art from the Dominican Republic and around the world. In addition to fine art, some specialty crafts are also sold on consignment here and it is a good place to find high-quality (albeit overpriced) Dominican handiwork. ⓐ Altos de Chavon ❶ 809 523 8470 ⓛ Open daily 09.30–19.00 ❶ Exhibits change monthly

Everett Designs Named for the designer and artisan Bill Everett, this jewellery shop is worth a mention for its gorgeous collection. Even if you are not in the market to buy, stop in to admire the suberb craftsmanship. ⓐ Altos de Chavon ❶ 809 523 8331 ⓛ Open Tues–Sat 10.00–19.00

NIGHTLIFE

Estudio 2000 Discotec This is a low-key dance club with a bar that is usually packed. ⓐ Avenida Santa Rosa 63 ❶ 809 813 0481 ⓛ Open nightly from 22.00

Intimo Piano Bar This is a small bar with, as the name implies, a cozy atmosphere. ⓐ Calle 1ra 67, Los Colonos ❶ 809 813 4198 ⓛ Open nightly from 18.00

◔ *Punta Caña's beach zone has a wide range of activities*

Punta Caña
beach-lover's paradise

Heavily influenced by the large number of European travellers, Punta Caña is mostly made up of resort hotels lined up along the beach. In contrast to some other resort locations, there is less segregation between tourists and locals here – that is to say, since there is no original town that was overrun by a giant hotel, the establishments are not obsessed with keeping locals out of their tennis courts and off their beaches. Punta Caña sits at the eastern end of Hispañiola and is most revered for its perfect, soft white sand.

The resort-made beach zone is popular with Latin Americans and Spanish as well as celebrities – Julio Iglesias often stays in his villa here. Punta Caña has its own airport, or can easily be accessed by bus from other regions. This area is packed with activities, ranging from casinos and nightclubs to plenty of water sports and relaxing time for sunbathing. It is a good town for those who prefer to have all amenities at their fingertips and do not want the hassle of looking about for something to do. There is always a party and never a dull moment along the beach, yet the town is not known for being rowdy or rough.

For those who are just passing through and would like to get a glimpse of the well-known beaches without booking at a mega-hotel or perhaps as a break from the frenzy of the high life, there is one public access beach. Located at **Cortecito**, it is far more relaxed than the rest of the area. Here you will find local beachgoers and adventurous Europeans taking a dip to cool off. If you are looking for a truly rustic getaway, try the little fishing town of **Juanillo**, 6 km (4 miles) south of Punta Caña.

THINGS TO SEE & DO
Diving ★★★
Scuba Caribe SA Five locations in Punta Caña offering lessons and rentals for beginners as well as experienced scuba divers.
ⓐ Carretera Friusa 1 ⓣ 809 221 1336/809 552 0379

Horse riding ★★★

Rancho RN-23 Over 100 horses to choose from at three ranches, the operation offers guided tours throughout the area. ⓐ Arena Gorda ⓣ 809 552 1529/809 747 7538

Outback Jungle Safari ★★★

This day-long tour may not be what many expect from its exotic name. Instead, tour operators pick you up from your hotel and will spend the day showing guests around the countryside by truck, exposing visitors to the real lives of the Dominican people. Some of the places visited include a school where visitors can speak to the local students, and you also get the chance to visit a market, and see how vanilla and coffee are produced. Meals and drinks (including rum) are included in the price of the day, plus siesta in a hammock. ⓐ Plaza Turisol, Local 7, Avenida Luperon ⓣ 809 244 4886 (north coast) or 809 552 0665 ⓦ www.outback-safaris.com ⓘ Admission charge; tours by booking, ages 12 and over

RESTAURANTS

 Capitán Cook €€€ This place specializes in grilled seafood and beachside views. ⓐ Marina ed Cortecito ⓣ 809 552 0645 ⓛ Open daily noon–midnight ⓘ Reservations are needed for those who are not hotel guests

NIGHTLIFE

Bavaro Disco This European-style disco with a state-of-the-art sound system is known for its loud music and scantily clad clientele, and is one of the most popular nightclubs in the area. ⓐ Bavaro Barcelo Beach, Golf & Casino Resort ⓣ 809 686 5797 ⓛ Open nightly 23.00–05.00 ⓘ Admission charged for those not staying at the resort

Samaná Peninsula &
Santa Barbara de Samaná
a naturalist's paradise

**For many travellers, the Samaná Peninsula is the ideal retreat. With
a setting no less perfect than the other resorts, this area's white sands
and turquoise waters have more space and more to see. The region has
become well known for its whale watching, especially for those who
like to view the humpback during its winter migration. The Samaná
Peninsula is also home to Parqué Nacional los Haitises (see page 80),
one of the most visited wildlife sanctuaries in the country.**

Natural wonders are revered by the residents of the peninsula, and there
has been a significant effort in this area in particular to encourage the
idea of sustainable tourism. In this way, visitors and Dominicans can
work together to maintain the land and the things the tourists have
come to see, so that the industry will not destroy itself. Many farmers
and locals on the peninsula are guides (also known as *paradas*) and

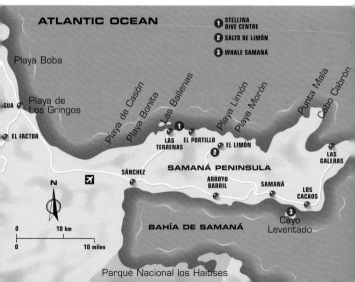

1 MOTO MARINA CLUB
2 WHALE SAMANÁ
3 MOTO MARINA WHALE WATCHING
4 DIVE SAMANÁ

LA CHURCHA †

CALLE SANTA BARBARA

CALLE MARIA TRINIDAD SÁNCHEZ

AVENIDA F DE ROSARIO SANC

SANTA BARBARA DE SAMANÁ (SAMANÁ)

AVDA F DE ROSARIO SÁNCHEZ (C5)

AVENIDA LA MARINA (MALECÓN)

SAMANÁ PORT

N

0   200 m
0   200 yds

Cayo Linares

Cayo Vigia

THE BRIDGE TO NOWHERE

Playa Escondido

BAHÍA DE SAMANÁ

craftspeople who will share the natural wonders of the landscape at an absurdly small fee. An astounding number of gorgeous waterfalls are among some of the most popular destinations.

Not all of the Samaná peninsula is made up of small towns and jungles, however. The city of **Santa Barbara de Samaná** (known as Samaná) has its own share of lively bustle, especially along its Malecón. Offering its share of restaurants and nightlife, it allows the naturalist the opportunity to unwind after a day of hiking with some merengue and rum. Since this well-protected port is the central point for the bay's whale watching industry, it becomes quite busy from January through to March while the whale population is high off its coast. During these months, the pace picks up significantly at the clubs along the Malecón, and those planning to visit should make reservations well in advance.

THINGS TO SEE & DO

La Churcha
(First African Wesleyan Methodist Church of Samaná) ★★

This historic building, brought to the island by the English as a mission attempt by the Methodists in 1823, is now a makeshift museum about the area's slave trade and local African culture. ⓐ Calle Santa Bárbara and Calle Duarte ⓒ Open daily 09.00–18.00 ⓘ No admission charge

⬥ Enjoy the natural wonders of the Samaná Peninsula

DIVE HOT SPOTS

The Tower 50 m (165 ft) of this 55 m (180 ft) mountain is under water, rich with amazing sea life.

La Catedral An enormous, underwater cave that has created an air pocket.

Plaza Monica Advanced divers can reach this reef – 30 m (100 ft) down – that houses large, bright sea life.

Cabo Cabrón Known as a spot where divers might hear the eerie songs of migrating whales.

Diving ★★★

Dive Samaná This outfit offers rentals and transportation to many great diving locations in the area. ❸ Casa Marina Bay Resort ❶ 809 538 0210 ❶ Open daily ❶ Admission charge

Stellina Dive Centre Coordinates dive trips to both popular and little-known spots in the region. ❸ Hotel Cacao Beach, Las Terrenas ❶ 809 240 6000 ❶ Excursions by reservation

Water sports ★★

Moto Marina Club This club offers rentals and instruction in snorkelling, kayaking, or paddleboat, as well as round-trip transportation services to Cayo Levantado. ❸ Avenida Malecón 3 ❶ 809 538 2302 ❸ motomarina@yahoo.com ❶ Open daily by schedule

Waterfalls ★★★

Waterfalls are usually toured with the aid of guides known as *paradas*. They may offer a meal or snack, show you crafts or a product that they and family members have made to sell, or simply offer to bring you to your destination. You may also choose to walk there yourself, but the trails can be difficult and steep and the fees for the *paradas'* ride on a horse or mule are very small in relation, so their services are recommended. You can also arrange to have a traditional meal waiting for you on your return.

Salto de Limón (Limón Waterfall) This is the most well-known waterfall in the region, with a drop of 46 m (150 ft) into a deep pool with lush, tropical surroundings. All trails that lead to the falls are maintained by the Association for Community Ecotourism of Salto del Limón (ACESAL). Trails sprout off from the road between Las Terrenas and Samaná, and along here you will find the many guides offering their services. Some of the more established *paradas* include Parada La Familia, Parada Ismael, Parada Santi, Parada Nega and Parada La Manzana. Many who are not listed are respected guides as well.

Whale watching ★★★

From mid-January to late March, several thousand humpback whales make their way to the temperate waters around the island, where the females give birth and the yearly mating takes place. Hopeful bull whales show off to prospective mates, and make a great show for the whale watchers, too. It is an impressive sight, and an excellent opportunity to witness the interactions and rituals of these ancient giants.

Whale Samaná & Victoria Marine Operated by Kim Bedall, known as one of the pioneers of the local whale watching industry. Two departure points offered, operating from 15 January–20 March: ➌ Avenida la Marina (Malecón) (🕿 809 538 2494 🕐 Two tours daily, departing at 09.00 and 13.30) and ➋ Cayo Levantado (🕐 Two tours daily, departing at 09.30 and 14.00).

Moto Marina Whale Watching Tours Multilingual staff provide an accompanying narration on boat excursions to watch the humpback migration. Moto Marina also offers round-trip transportation services to Cayo Levantado. ➋ Avenida la Marina (Malecón) 3 🕿 809 538 2302 ✉ motomarina@yahoo.com 🕐 Whale watching tours operating daily, 15 January–25 March ❶ Admission charge

RESTAURANTS & BARS (see map on page 40)

Café de Paris € ❶ Excellent pizzas, operated by French owners in a relaxed atmosphere. ⓐ Avenida la Marina (Malecón) 6 ⓣ 809 538 2257 ⓛ Open daily 10.00–midnight

Camilo Malecón € ❷ Traditional Dominican meals right on the water. ⓐ Avenida la Marina (Malecón) ⓛ Open daily 10.00–23.00

La Hacienda €–€€ ❸ Known for steaks and French cuisine in a lovely outdoor café setting. ⓐ E de Leon 6 ⓣ 809 538 2383 ⓛ Open daily for lunch and dinner

Restaurante Chino € ❹ Typical Chinese food for take-out or dining in. ⓐ T Chasereaux ⓣ 809 538 2215 ⓛ Open daily 14.00–midnight

NIGHTLIFE

Anyeli Café Club € ❺ Full bar also offering light food and music. ⓐ Calle Ppal 25 ⓣ 809 538 0053

La Loba € ❻ With more local clientele, a laid-back atmosphere and large crowds every night. ⓐ Avenida F de Rosario Sánchez (C5) ⓛ Open nightly 21.00–04.00 ⓘ Cover charge

Naomi €€ ❼ Techno-mix club with some latin music. ⓐ E De Leon 4 ⓛ Open nightly 23.00–05.00

Rancho Allegre €€ ❽ Popular venue featuring outdoor dancing to traditional Dominican merengue music. ⓐ Avenida la Marina (Malecón) ⓛ Open nightly 22.00–04.00

◗ *Whale watching in the waters around the peninsula is a popular activity*

Cabarete
the city that sails

Just 20 km (12 miles) from Puerto Plata Airport, this town has become a mecca for windsurfers and kiteboarders. Its white sand beaches combined with near-perfect breezes create ideal conditions for both the first-time windsurfer and the expert water-sports enthusiast. The nightlife is equally exciting, with plenty of restaurants and clubs to choose from right along the waterfront. Almost all of the town's action happens along the Calle Principal, or Carretera 5, and the beach it runs parallel to, and it serves as a starting point for many of the region's adventurous excursions, such as hiking and canyoning. Cabarete is most popular with the young and active crowd.

The best time for the novice windsurfer to hit the waves in Cabarete is in the morning, when the breezes are lighter and the water is calmer. One might also feel less self-conscious during the earlier hours when trying to learn the ropes, since the wind picks up as the day progresses and the beach begins to fill with people. Spectators come to watch the more experienced windsurfers, who take full advantage of the trade winds that blow in late in the day.

Kiteboarding is the newest sport to hit the waves, and is popular with young people for its flexibility and stunts. Cabarete is filled with plenty of shops that offer instruction and rentals, and has recently become host to yearly international kiteboarding championships, where spectators can watch some amazing feats performed on the water, including jumps and flips that could never be accomplished with windsurfing.

THINGS TO SEE & DO
Diving ★

Hippocampo Dive Centre Individual and group diving classes for beginners and those who need to touch up on skills are offered, as well as a good selection of rentals and equipment for sale. ⓐ Calle Principal (Carretera 5), next to Tropicana Club Hotel ⓣ 809 571 0956

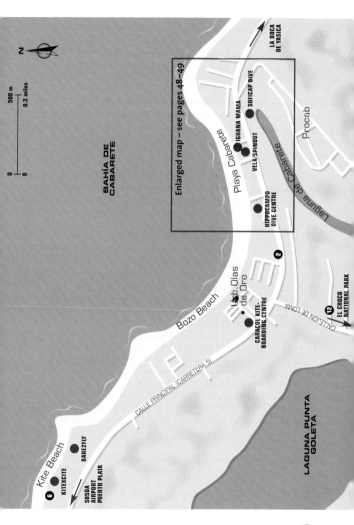

N

BAHÍA DE CABARETE

0
0

500 m
0.3 miles

LA BOCA DE YASICA

SOFICAP DIVE

IGUANA MAMA

Playa Cabarete

VELA/SPINOUT

Procab

Laguna Cabarete

Enlarged map – see pages 48–49

HIPPOCAMPO DIVE CENTRE

Bozo Beach

Lab.Olas de Oro

CARACOL KITE-BOARDING CENTRE

2

CALLEJÓN DE LOMA

EL CHOCO NATIONAL PARK

12

CALLE PRINCIPAL (CARRETERA 5)

Kite Beach

6

KITEXCITE

DARE2FLY

SOSÚA AIRPORT PUERTO PLATA

LAGUNA PUNTA GOLETA

Soficap This company offers diving equipment rentals and instruction for the Cabarete beach area. ➊ Calle Principal (Carretera 5) ➊ 809 571 0280 ➍ Open daily by appointment

Hiking and adventure tours ★★★
Iguana Mama A nationally recognized group of naturalists and guides who offer hiking opportunities to Mount Isabela and Pico Duarte, as well as mountain bike rentals and tours, cultural tours, canyoning and rafting trips, diving instruction and horse riding. ➊ Calle Principal 74 (Carretera 5) ➊ 809 571 0908/571 0228 ➌ www.iguanamama.com

El Choco National Park One of the destinations of Iguana Mama and other local tour operators, the park is best viewed with a guide to truly

appreciate its treasures and avoid becoming lost in its maze of jungles, caves, and lagoons mapped out by poorly marked paths. Home to thousands of birds, El Choco National Park is a stunning place where visitors can see hills that were once undersea coral reefs and visit underground pools in caves that still boast Taino petroglyphs. The park used to be called the Area Protegida Cabarete y Goleta, named for its two lagoons. ● Callejon de la Loma ● Open Mon–Fri 09.00–17.00 ● Entrance fee

Kiteboarding ★ ★ ★
Caracol Kiteboarding Center Operated by champion windsurfer and kiteboarder Laurel Eastman, this school offers classes for the everyone, from beginner and intermediate, to even the experienced kitesurfer.

HIPPOCAMPO DIVE CENTRE ●

⓫

● SOFICAP DIVE

LAGUNA DE CABARETE

Procab

🔺 *Cabarete offers excellent windsurfing opportunities*

ⓐ Urbanacion Olas de Oro 1 at the Aparthotel Caracol ⓣ 809 571 0680
ⓦ www.hotelcaracol.com/kite ⓛ Open daily

Dare2Fly Offers kiteboarding equipment rentals and lessons for
beginners. ⓐ Office at Calle Principal 1 (Carretera 5), lessons at Kitexcite
Beach ⓣ 809 571 0787/0805 ⓛ Open daily ⓘ Rental fees

Kitexcite These kiteboarding lessons offer a unique system of radio
communication within helmets so the instructors can give immediate
feedback while you are on the water. ⓐ Kitexcite Beach ⓣ 809 571
9509/9732 ⓛ Open daily for lessons, 09.00–17.00 for phone inquiries

Windsurfing ★★
Vela/Spinout Highly regarded windsurfing outfitter that offers
equipment rentals with optional insurance and classes. ⓐ Calle Principal
1 (Carretera 5), same location as Dare2Fly office (see above) ⓣ 809
571 0787/0805 ⓘ Free windsurfing clinics offered daily; lessons by
appointment for a fee

RESTAURANTS & BARS (see maps pages 47, 48–49)

The heavy influx of European expats to the area has had a wonderful influence on the culinary selection available to visitors. Many of the town's restaurants are owned and operated by Germans, British, French, Swiss, Italians and others, all of whom contribute to one of the greatest varieties you will find in the country.

Las Brisas €–€€ ❶ (see pages 48–49) Decent food and very popular dance club serving up local music and European techno beats. ❸ Calle Principal (Carretera 5) ❶ 809 571 0614 ❶ Open for lunch and dinner; bar and club open until 05.00

Cabarete Blud € ❷ (see page 47) This informal place is open for light meals and snacks. ❸ Calle Principal 30 (Carretera 5) ❶ 809 571 9714 ❶ Open daily 10.00–22.00

Cana Tropical €€ ❸ (see pages 48–49) International cuisine specializing in fresh seafood, with a wide variety of music including reggae, soul, and jazz. ❸ Calle Principal and Calle Iguana Mama ❶ 809 571 0101/499 1049 ❶ Open for lunch and dinner until 02.00; happy hour from midnight to 01.00 every Friday night

Casa del Pescador €€ ❹ (see pages 48–49) A romantic setting on the beach, serving the day's catch of seafood. ❸ Calle Principal (Carretera 5) ❶ Open nightly 18.00–midnight

Comedor Hebrero € ❺ (see pages 48–49) Fried chicken and other fast food: eat in or take out. ❸ Carretera C Sabaneta 180, off Calle Principal (Carretera 5) ❶ 809 571 0712 ❶ Open daily noon–23.00

Extreme Restaurant € ❻ (see page 47) Specializes in Asian dishes with mixed menu and buffet. ❸ Calle Principal (Carretera 5) ❶ 809 571 0880 ❶ Open daily for breakfast, lunch and dinner

Lax €€ **7** (see pages 48–49) A bar and nightclub named for its relaxed atmosphere and general philosophy. It also serves breakfast, lunch and dinner and specializes in sushi. ⓐ Calle Principal (Carretera 5) ⓣ 809 571 0042 ⓛ Open 24 hours

Miro's €€€ **8** (see pages 48–49) Miro's offers an expensive but excellent imported wine selection to accompany fine seafood with a Mediterranean flare. The restaurant walls act as a gallery for up-and-coming artists. ⓐ Calle Principal (Carretera 5) ⓣ 809 571 0888 ⓛ Open daily 11.00–13.00 and 19.00–midnight

Ocean Taste Restaurant €€ **9** (see pages 48–49) Seafood so fresh that you may have snorkelled past it earlier in the day. ⓐ Calle Principal (Carretera 5) ⓣ 809 571 0430 ⓛ Open daily for lunch and dinner

Panadería Repostera Dick € **10** (see pages 48–49) Pastries and breads, fresh squeezed juices, and coffee. ⓐ Calle Principal (Carretera 5) ⓣ 809 571 1507 ⓛ Open daily 05.00–noon

La Pizzería De Cabarete € **11** (see pages 48–49) A typical pizzeria, conveniently located in the centre of town. ⓐ Calle Principal (Carretera 5) ⓣ 809 571 0888 ⓛ Open daily noon–02.00

El Tiguerre € **12** (see page 47) A truly authentic Dominican experience, just outside of town. ⓐ Callejon de la Loma ⓣ No telephone ⓛ Open for lunch

Vento €€ **13** (see pages 48–49) Italian restaurant in a great, central location. ⓐ Calle Principal 39 (Carretera 5) ⓣ 809 571 0977/805 3377 ⓔ vento@cabareterestaurants.com ⓛ Open nightly, evenings only

Sosúa
cultural melting pot

The charming diver's hotspot of Sosúa was founded as a refugee settlement for about 600 Jewish Germans escaping from the Nazi persecution during World War II. Although it was an attempt to make himself look better after a mass slaughter of Haitians on his own island, Dominican dictator Rafael Trujillo was one of the few leaders at the time who allowed Jewish refugees to freely come to his country. The group developed the land, most notably creating a small dairy farming industry, and are known for their fine smoked meats. Despite the country's overwhelming percentage of Roman Catholics, the townspeople of Sosúa have never been met with discrimination. This has given the town a certain draw for Europeans and lends to its continental ambience.

In addition to its international flare, Sosúa is regarded as a growing centre for water sports, especially diving. Its picturesque and inviting beach perfectly resembles a crescent moon, and is tipped with rock structures that extend out into the sea. Surfers and sunbathers enjoy this secluded area, and there are plenty of places to take out a sailboat or go for a jet-ski.

Sosúa is a diver's paradise, and is certainly the place to go if you are looking for some spectacular dive sites. The waters around the town boast some incredible coral reefs and ocean life that can be easily accessed. Many dive spots are suitable for both beginners and experts, with several levels of treasure to uncover. One of the most fascinating spots is the sunken cargo ship *Zingara*, which plummeted to a depth of 36 m (118 ft). Even here, the less experienced can explore the shallow reef wall above and enjoy the fan corals and tube sponges that make it their home.

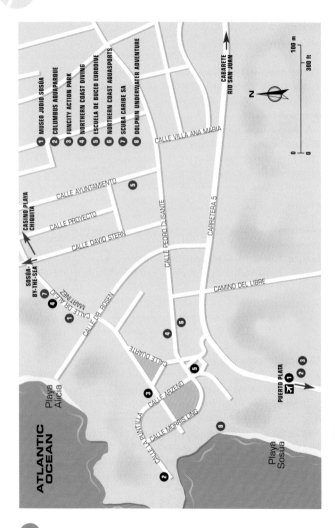

1 MUSEO JUDIO SOSÚA
2 COLUMBUS AQUAPARQUE
3 FUNCITY ACTION PARK
4 NORTHERN COAST DIVING
5 ESCUELA DE BUCEO EURODIVE
6 NORTHERN COAST AQUASPORTS
7 SCUBA CARIBE SA
8 DOLPHIN UNDERWATER ADVENTURE

ATLANTIC OCEAN

Playa Alicia

Playa Sosúa

CALLE VILLA ANA MARIA

CALLE AYUNTAMIENTO

CALLE PROYECTO

CALLE DAVID STERN

CALLE PEDRO CLISANTE

CARRETERA 5

CAMINO DEL LIBRE

CALLE DR ALEJO MARTINEZ

CALLE DR ROSEN

CALLE DUARTE

CALLE ARZENO

CALLE LA PUNTILLA

CALLE MORRIS LING

CASINO PLAYA CHIQUITA

SOSÚA-BY-THE-SEA

CABARETE RIO SAN JUAN

PUERTO PLATA

N

0   100 m
0   300 ft

THINGS TO SEE & DO

Casino Playa Chiquita ★

Full-service casino offering 96 gaming machines and seven gaming tables. Also on the premises are a gift shop, restaurant, swimming pool, nightclub and full amenities to keep guests spending. ⓐ Isabel la Católica ⓣ 809 571 3416 ⓒ Open 24 hours

Columbus Aquaparque ★★

Large water park equipped with a wide range of rides to satisfy the swimmers, as well as shops, restaurants, and bars to keep the land-goers content. ⓐ Playa Sosúa ⓣ 809 571 2642 or 571 2254 ⓒ Open daily 10.00–18.00 ⓘ Admission charge

Diving ★★

Escuela de Buceo Eurodive ⓐ Ayuntamiento 44 ⓣ 809 571 1093
ⓔ eurodive@verizon.net.do
Dolphin Underwater Adventure Playa Sosúa 45 ⓣ 809 571 0842
Northern Coast Aquasports ⓐ Avenida Pedro Clisante 5 ⓣ 809 571 1028
Northern Coast Diving ⓐ Avenida Pedro Clisante 8 ⓣ 809 571 1028
ⓦ www.northerncoastdiving.com
Scuba Caribe SA ⓐ Calle Dr A Martínez ⓣ 809 571 1014

FunCity Action Park ★★

Go-carts, bumper cars, grand prix and more, plus a special kiddie section for ages 2–8. Food and beverages on site, and shuttle services to and from Sosúa and other nearby towns provided. ⓐ Carretera 5 (Puerto Plata, Km 5) ⓣ 809 320 1031 ⓦ www.funcity-gocarts.com ⓒ Open daily ⓘ Admission charge

Museo Judio Sosúa (Hebrew Colony Museum) ★

Set up by the refugees during World War II, this museum features exhibits on local Jewish colonies. ⓐ Calle Dr A Martínez and Calle Dr Rosen ⓣ 809 571 1386 ⓒ Open Mon–Fri 09.00–13.00 and 14.00–16.00; call ahead for groups ⓘ Admission charge

RESTAURANTS (see map on page 54)

Comedor Pica Pollo el Nuevo Día € ❶ Traditional Dominican fried chicken spot. ⓐ General G Luperón 5 ☎ 809 571 3823 🕒 Open daily 10.00–22.00

La Puntilla de Piergiorgio €€ ❷ Specializing in fresh seafood and Italian entrées. Boasts several patios that overlook Sosúa's scenic bay ⓐ Calle La Puntilla (at the Piergiorgio Palace Hotel) ☎ 809 571 2626/2215 🕒 Open daily noon–23.00

Restaurant Pizzeria Da'Alberto € ❸ Typical pizzeria with in-house dining. ⓐ Calle Dr A Martínez 53 ☎ 809 571 2069 🕒 Open daily 10.00–23.00

Tainobeach €–€€ ❹ This restaurant and bar serves up seafood, steaks, and pizza in a funky round hut. ⓐ El Batey, next to Casa Marina Beach Hotel ☎ 809 571 1269 🕒 Open daily for lunch and dinner; bar open until 04.00

DIVE SITES

If you're an experienced diver and want to see the best of the region or you're learning but want to get the most of you trip, here are the places to ask about first:

Paradise Reef Novices will enjoy the bright coral reef at about 12 m (39 ft), while experts can visit octopus and squid at 32 m (105 ft).

Garden of Los Charamicaos Large sponges and bright fan corals adorn this site, reaching a maximum depth of 24 m (79 ft).

Pyramids A beautiful result of erosion, go 15 m (49 ft) down through and between the corals.

Airport Wall Considered one of the best spots, this 24 m (79 ft) deep area has several caves and elkhorn coral.

NIGHTLIFE

Voodoo Lounge ❺ This disco declares itself 'a step up', although it still draws in a heavy drinking crowd. ⓐ Calle Pedro Clisante, by the Sosúa Bay Hotel ❶ 809 571 3559 ⓛ Open nightly 17.00–05.00

⬥ Sosúa Beach is shaped like a perfect crescent moon

Punta
Fortaleza

FUERTE DE
SAN FELIPE

BAHÍA DE
PUERTO
PLATA

N

0   25
0   500 ft

AVENIDA GENERAL LÓPEZ

CALLE SANCHEZ

MALECÓN

4

CALLE 30 DE MARZO

CALLE 12 DE JULIO

3

CALLE J. F. KENNEDY

CALLE BELLER

† PARQUE
CENTRAL

CALLE DUARTE

PARQUE

LO
BEA

CALLE 16 DE AGOSTO

CALLE 20 DE DICIEMBRE

AVENIDA SEPARACIÓN

CALLE LUIS ESPINOSA

CALLE CASTELLANOS

MUSEO
DE ÁMBAR

OLD CITY

CALLE ANTERA MOTA

CALLE FRANCISCO J

CALLE 2

CALLE EL MORRO

CALLE 4

CALLE 6

CALLE 6

VILLA NUEVA

MERCADO

AV. 27 DE FEBRERO

AV VIRGINIA ORTEGA

CALLE 2

C. PRESID

CALLE 1

AVENIDA COLÓN

CALLE 30 DE MARZO

CALLE
ALTAGRACIA

AV. ISABEL DE TORRES

CALLE JUAN LAFITTI

CALLE CAMINO REAL

CALLE J. KUNHARDT

CALLE 5

AVENIDA PEDRO CLISANTE

Arroyo los Montones

OCEAN WORLD
CABLE CAR RIDE
LA ISABELA

AVENIDA JOSÉ
GINEBRA

AVENIDA CIRCUNVALACIÓN SUR

PL
B
BOTT

1

Puerto Plata & Playa Dorada
cultural hotspot

The city of Puerto Plata is a thriving metropolis supported both by tourism and the rum and tobacco industries. Those seeking out the historical richness of one of the very first European settlements of the New World will adore the Old City, and anyone looking for more excitement and bustle will enjoy the New City. Visitors looking for package-type resort holidays flock to Playa Dorada, which is close enough to be part of the city yet is literally walled off from Puerto Plata. The region as a whole is one of the hottest spots in the country for nightlife and culture.

The Old City of Puerto Plata sits on the east side of town, beginning at the corner of Avenida Separacion and Beller. Its atmosphere is elegant yet rustic, a memory of the days when it was the centre of a prosperous Victorian town. The architecture reflects both the era and the former wealth of its residents, and includes a grand, gingerbread-sytle mansion. A stroll along the Parque Central, located just south of the Malecón, will give you a good look at the old homes of wealthy merchants and a two-storey gazebo in Victorian style, featuring Moorish arches. There are plentiful benches and shady spots for a relaxing break or picnic.

Public buses are an inexpensive way to get from one end of town to the other and regularly bring passengers from the far end of the Malecón to the Parque Central, but they make frequent stops and can take nearly an hour and a half for one round trip. The bus is, however, still a sensible and affordable alternative for those visiting Playa Dorada on a day pass. Walking is the best option for getting around the most-visited areas of the city, since most sights are close to each other. Taxis are, as usual, a more expensive alternative, but are well worth taking for a trip that requires going any distance through the barrios or less-developed areas.

THINGS TO SEE & DO
Brugal Rum Bottling Plant ★★
Free guided tours of the bottling process are given to visitors, as well as a fresh daiquiri. ⓐ Highway 5 (Beller 4) ⓣ 809 586 2531 ⓛ Open Mon–Fri 08.00–15.00, closed Sat–Sun ⓘ No admission charge

Cable car ride ★★★
This 25-minute ride to the top of Mount Isabela should not be missed. The views from the top are lovely, and you can see the city and the coast-line below. ⓐ Circunvalación Sur on Avenida Teleférico ⓛ Operates Mon–Sat 08.30–15.30, closed Sun ⓘ Admission charge

Fuerta de San Felipe (San Felipe Fort) ★★
One of the first forts to be built after European arrival, this grand edifice has proven itself able to withstand even the most brutal of attacks. It has 2.5 m (8 ft) thick walls and a deep moat, and will bring out the adventurer in anyone. The turrets can be climbed, the old prison rooms may be toured and there is plenty to learn in the on-site museum from the fort's weapons collection and biographies of past residents such as Juan Pablo Duarte. ⓐ Avenida Colon, Puerto Plata ⓣ 809 261 6043 ⓛ Open Thurs–Tues 09.00–noon and 14.00–17.00; closed Wed ⓘ Admission charge

Long Beach ★★
Beach-goers will find the merengue loud and vibrant down on Long Beach, which is the official beginning of Puerto Plata's Malecón. This is a public beach, and is popular with sunbathers and party-goers. It has also been known as a good place to spot whales during their winter migration. Night time on this beach does get a bit seedy however, so do not be surprised if you are approached by prostitutes after dark.

Malecón ★★★
Puerto Plata's Malecón is one of the hippest in the country, extending 2 km (1 mile) from Long Beach to Avenida Hermanas Mirabal. It is a

◆ *Beautiful views around Puerto Plata*

popular daytime boardwalk with shops, restaurants, and tourist vendors selling everything from fried plantains and chicken to handmade jewellery and souvenirs. The bars along the seaside strip open up in the evening (although alcoholic beverages can be bought nearly any time of day), and by sundown the beach party is in full force.

Museo de Ambar (Amber Museum) ★ ★ ★

One of the two major museums in the country dedicated to this fossilized resin, this collection is the result of three decades' dedication by the Costa family. Some of the more fantastic pieces include leaves and flowers from the Triassic and Jurassic periods, and a lizard that has been perfectly preserved for several million years. Many of the pieces of amber in the collection contain insects, plant life, water or air as old as 60 million years. The museum is spread out over two floors of the Villa Berz mansion, a stunning architectural feat in its own right. ⓐ Calle Duarte and Calle Castellanos ⓣ 809 586 2848 ⓛ Open Mon–Sat 09.00–18.00, closed Sun ⓘ Admission charge

● *Buy a day pass for Playa Dorada and enjoy a five-star day*

Ocean World ★ ★ ★

This immense water park enthralls both adults and children alike, combining the fun of water play with the fascination of viewing exotic animals. This park's claim to fame is the pool where you can actually swim with sharks – obviously ones that won't eat you! Another big attraction is a plexiglass window that allows you to swim past tigers. The park also offers the chance to swim with dolphins, sea lions and many bright exotic fish. In addition, a large marina is under construction at this site. ❸ Ppal 2 Cofresí ❶ 809 291 1111 ⓦ www.ocean-world.info ⏾ Open daily ❶ Admission charge; additional charges for animal encounters

EXCURSIONS

La Isabela ★

Named after the Queen of Spain, this site was the second official settlement of Columbus in the New World. Recently designated a national park, this site does not have much left in the way of original structures from 1494 but has maintained its original rustic charm. Stones still map out the border of the humble church that held the first Catholic Mass of the New World, and there are other buildings that can be traced out by their foundations. A museum has been set up to display artefacts found at the site and it includes both weapons and daily items from Columbus' 1200 men, as well as many Taino items. A cemetery is also located nearby, where the remains of a Spanish soldier have been excavated for display. To visit La Isabela, it is best to plan your trip with a tour operator within the city rather than to rent a car to make the two-and-a-half-hour drive from Puerto Plata yourself, even if it looks simple enough on a map. Road conditions in the area make the journey treacherous at best, and it is best done in professional vehicles.

Playa Dorada ★

If you want to hang out at the exclusive beach without buying a package at one of the 14 all-inclusives, consider getting a day pass from any one of the hotels located at Playa Dorada. The walled-in complex boasts a huge beach, golfing, tennis, dancing, and lessons for a wide variety of water sports like snorkelling and water skiing. Conveniences include several banks, a department store, a travel agency and a medical centre. Night time at the compound is just as exciting, when three casinos light up the sky and dozens of bars, restaurants and discos keep things alive until the early morning hours. This is also a boutique mecca, with nearly 100 shops to choose from. ⓐ Playa Dorada is on Cerretera 5, about 1 km (½ mile) east of Puerto Plata

RESTAURANTS (see map on page 58)

Café Cito €€ ❶ A truly unique dining experience – you may want to play on the trampoline before you have the decadent fillet mignon! You can also relax and enjoy the jazz and blues, or play in the shallow pool. ⓐ Within walking distance from Playa Dorada, Sosúa highway, Km 4 ❶ 809 586 7923

Pizzeria Internacional €€ ❷ Serves the expected fare as well as fresh seafood. ⓐ Avenida Hermamas Miribal ❶ 809 586 4740 🕒 Open for lunch and dinner

Sam's Bar & Grill € ❸ The hotel itself is worth a visit for its architectural grandeur. It was built in the 1890s and is proudly known as the city's first hotel. Serves American favourites such as Philly cheese-steak. ⓐ José del Carmen Ariza 34 at Hotel Castilla ❶ 809 586 7267 🕒 Open daily 07.00–23.00

NIGHTLIFE

Discoteca Orión ❹ Very popular dance club, especially for merengue and bachata dance. ⓐ Calle 30 de Marzo 20, Puerto Plata ❶ 809 320 8956 🕒 Open nightly 19.00–05.00

Hemingway's Bar & Grill ❺ Also serving meals, this high-end hot spot can get rowdy by early morning. ⓐ Playa Dorada Plaza ❶ 809 320 2230 🕒 Open daily 11.00–05.00

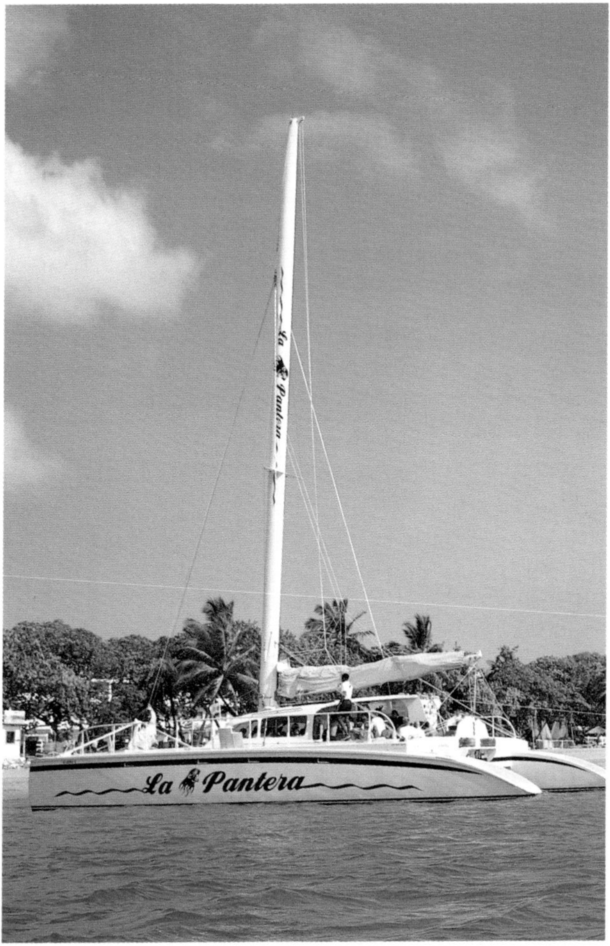

State-of-the-art yachts line the beach at Playa Dorada

Santiago
merengue town

This former mining town is one of the few inland cities that still has a great nightlife and a healthy stream of visitors. It is famed as a major tobacco exporter, but more importantly as the home of the Dominican merengue. Known on the island as *merengue périco ripao*, the music for this dance is traditionally played with the *guira*, *tambora* and the accordian. As a result of the local pride in musical heritage, there are plenty of dance clubs that are lively all night.

Although taxis are readily available (try **Camino** ✆ 809 971 7788), the city's main points of interest are mostly within walking distance and never more than a few blocks from the downtown parks.

◆ *The bright lights of Santiago*

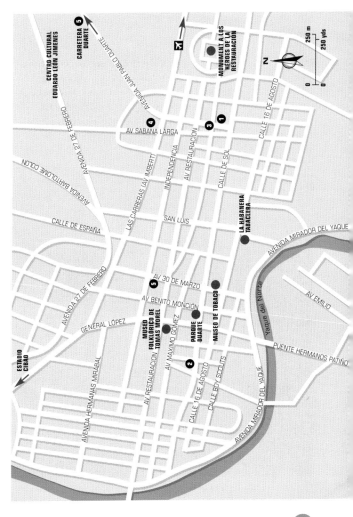

CENTRO CULTURAL
EDUARDO LEÓN JIMENES

CARRETERA
DUARTE 5

MONUMENTA A LOS
HÉROES DE LA
RESTAURACIÓN

250 m
250 yds

N

AVENIDA JUAN PABLO DUARTE

CALLE 16 DE AGOSTO

4 AV. SABANA LARGA

3 1

AVENIDA 27 DE FEBRERO

INDEPENDENCIA

AV. RESTAURACIÓN

CALLE DE SOL

AVENIDA BARTOLOME COLON

LAS CARRERAS (AV. IMBERT)

SAN LUIS

CALLE DE ESPAÑA

LA HABANERA
TABACALERA

AVENIDA MIRADOR DEL YAQUE

AV 30 DE MARZO

5

AVENIDA 27 DE FEBRERO

AV. BENITO MONCIÓN

MUSEO DE TABACO

AV EMILIO

Yaque del Norte

GENERAL LÓPEZ

MUSEO
FOLKLÓRICO DE
TOMÁS MOREL

PARQUE
DUARTE

PUENTE HERMANOS PATIÑO

ESTADIO
CIBAO

AVENIDA HERMANAS MIRABAL

AV. RESTAURACIÓN

AV. MÁXIMO GÓMEZ

2

CALLE 16 DE AGOSTO

CALLE BOY SCOUTS

AVENIDA MIRADOR DEL YAQUE

67

⬤ Monument a los Héroes de la Restauración offers great views of the city

THINGS TO SEE & DO
Centro Cultural Eduardo León Jimenes ★★
This is a museum of both art and anthropology, containing Taino artefacts over 5000 years old. ⓐ Avenida 27 de Febrero 146 ⓣ 809 582 2315 ⓛ Open daily 09.00–17.00 ⓘ Free admission

Estadio Cibao ★★
Santiago's professional baseball stadium is filled with enthusiasts from November to February. Baseball fans in the area during the season should always be on the lookout for their favourite stars. ⓐ Avenida Imbert ⓛ See local newspapers for game times and ticket vendors

La Habanera Tabaclera (Cigar Factory) ★
The oldest cigar factory still operating in the country gives walk-through tours where aficionados can watch the entire process, beginning to end. ⓐ Calle 16 de Agosto and Calle San Luis ⓣ 809 580 4656 ⓔ info@latabacalera.com ⓛ Open, tours Mon–Fri 08.30–16.30 ⓘ Free admission

Monument a los Héroes de la Restauración (Monument to the Heroes of the Restoration) ★★
Originally built in 1940 by Rafael Trujillo in honor of himself, this impressive tower now commemorates the War of Independence from Spain. If you can make it up the stairs to the top of the 70 m (230 ft) monument, the views of the city are spectacular. ⓐ Avenida Monumental ⓛ Open Mon–Sat 09.00–noon and 14.00–17.00, closed Sun ⓘ Free admission

Museo Folklórico de Tomas Morel (Tomas Morel Museum of Folk Art) ★★
A bright and festive collection of carnival masks is the main attraction here, as well as native Taino items and various relics from early Spanish settlers. ⓐ Calle Restauración 174 ⓣ 809 582 6787 ⓛ Open Mon–Fri 08.30–13.30 and 15.30–17.30 ⓘ Free admission

Museo de Tobaco (Tobacco Museum) ★
Exhibits in this Victorian building record the history of tobacco farming and use on the island from its earliest days with the native Taino.
ⓐ Calle 16 de Agosto and Calle 30 de Marzo ⏰ Open Tues–Fri 09.00–noon and 14.00–17.00, Sat 09.00–noon ⓘ Free admission

Parque Duarte ★★
An afternoon at the park would be incomplete without a ride in a horse-drawn carriage. Be sure to have the driver point out the 19th-century **Catedral de Santiago Apóstol** that sits alongside the park and is worth a visit for its stained glass and detailed mahogany carvings.

RESTAURANTS (see map on page 67)
El Café €€€ ❶ Excellent seafood and roasts in a very formal atmosphere. ⓐ Calle Texas and Calle 5 ☎ 809 587 4247 ⏰ Open nightly 17.00–23.00

Deli Pollo € ❷ Fried chicken eatery with no frills. ⓐ Avenida A Guzmán 141 ☎ 809 582 9878

Pizzeria Olé €–€€ ❸ Anticipated fare plus Dominican-style Creole cuisine in a unique, thatched-roof setting. ⓐ Avenida J P Duarte 30 ☎ 809 581 0410 ⏰ Open daily for lunch and dinner

NIGHTLIFE
Alcazar ❹ Known for not only the hot merengue but its party-until-breakfast momentum, this is one of the best dance clubs in Santiago. Don't expect any action here until at least 01.00. ⓐ Avenida E Sadhalá 10 (at Hotel El Gran Almirante) ☎ 809 580 1992 ⏰ Open nightly until 07.30

Club Nocturno Casa Blanca ❺ A popular nightclub that offers two locations and stays open as late (or as early) as the crowd will dance. ⓐ Las Aromas 2 ☎ 809 582 3790 ⓐ Carretera Duarte Km 5 ☎ 809 583 3075 ⏰ Open nightly from 22.00

⬥ Learn about the cigar-making process on a factory tour

La Vega
carnival central

February brings carnival time, and with it over 50,000 tourists to this otherwise rarely visited city. Twenty city blocks are reserved for the parade, where arguably some of the very best and most elaborate masks and costumes in the nation can be seen. In fact, those looking to bring home an authentic carnival devil-mask would find the 30 km (18½ mile) ride from Santiago worthwhile for the top-quality craftsmanship and La Vega name.

La Vega Vieja, which is situated about 5 km (3 miles) outside La Vega, is a national historic park set up on the ruins of Columbus' 1494 settlement. His travels inland were made in attempt to find Taino natives – unfortunately not for their cultural input, but for slavery. This was a thriving little town in its day, thanks to the discovery of gold nearby, but an earthquake levelled almost all of the buildings in 1562 and it was abandoned.

According to legend, a vision of the Virgin Mary appeared at a spot nearby, now known as **Santo Cerro** (Holy Hill). She is said to have appeared above a cross that Columbus buried in the ground during a battle with the Taino, which gave the Spanish the upper hand to win the battle. The **Iglesia Las Mercedes** is supposed to contain relics of this cross, and is visited each year in September in pilgrimage.

TO VISIT
To reach **La Vega Vieja** or **Santo Cerro** and **La Iglesia Las Mercedes**, either take Highway 1 northeast out of La Vega, or consider hiring a taxi or touring company.
Metro Taxi ❸ Calle M Gómez 22 ❶ 809 573 0303/3858
Taxi Del Cibao ❸ Calle Manz A Multif ❶ 809 573 0606/0200
Caribe Tours ❸ Carretera La Vega ❶ 809 573 3488

◆ *La Vega comes alive during the annual carnival*

RESTAURANTS & BARS

Café Claro Tropical Bar € Full bar with light lunch menu and sandwiches. ⓐ Avenida P A Rivera Km 0 ⓣ 809 573 9059 ⓛ Open daily 11.00–02.00

Express Hongri € Inexpensive, Dominican fast-food restaurant. ⓐ Avenida G Rivas 48 ⓣ 809 573 6953 ⓛ Open daily 10.00–midnight

Mariscos Del Atlántico €€ Fresh seafood brought in daily from the coast. ⓐ Calle Restauración 51 ⓣ 809 242 2832 ⓛ Open Mon–Sat for lunch and dinner

Panaderia–Pizzeria Las Palmas € Fresh baked breads and oven-baked pizzas. ⓐ Calle Batista 1 ⓣ 809 242 1212 ⓛ Open Mon–Sat 11.00–14.00 and 17.00–22.00, closed Sun

Pica Pollo El Buen Sabor € Sit-down fried chicken eatery. ⓐ General J Rodríguez 20 ⓣ 809 573 1097 ⓛ Open daily 10.00–22.00

Robert Restaurant Car Wash € This restaurant is above the car wash, not in it, and food is available for take away. ⓐ Autopista Duarte Km 1 ⓣ 809 573 0841 ⓛ Open daily for lunch and dinner

Jarabacoa
bustling mountain village

Best known as a starting point for hikes up Pico Duarte, Jarabacoa is a popular mountain resort for many Dominicans. Its cooler summer climate and pine-covered scenery make a lovely backdrop for whitewater rafting, canyoning and mountain biking. The town gained its moment of fame when one of its waterfalls, Salto Jimenoa, was featured in the film *Jurassic Park*. This is also a coffee-growing region, so be sure to sample the local goods.

Although set back in the interior of the island, this small city is busy enough to have all of the modern conveniences that most tourists require. If you are looking for a serene mountain village, you are likely be disappointed, however, by the bustle and pollution caused by numerous motorbikes and ATVs. But the Jarabacoa area is a fabulous place to experience plenty of adventure and outdoor activitiy at a pace much less stressful than a crowded beach town.

 For Internet, try **Net Café** – often crowded, but inexpensive and dependable. ❷ Parque Central, Fl 1 ● Open 09.00–01.00

GETTING AROUND
Please keep in mind that roads in this section of the country are notorious for being badly kept, and you may be well advised to let a local take you to your destinations.
Taxi Jarabacoa ❷ The taxi stand is at the corner of José Duran and Avenida Independencia, or you can call for service ● 809 574 7474
Francis Rent-a-Car ❷ Carretera a Salto Jimenoa Dos, Km 2
● 809 574 2981
Bus terminal Service to La Vega ❷ Avenida Independencia at José Duran

WATERFALLS

Salto Jimenoa When the water crashes from this 75 m (246 ft) fall, the mist produces rainbows, making this a truly amazing sight. ❸ The trail to the falls is off Carretera Constanza, about 7.5 km (4½ miles) south of Jarabacoa; the way is signposted – take care walking along the very steep path ❶ Admission free

Salto Jimenoa I or Lower Salto Jimenoa This waterfall is much easier to get to, but is often quite crowded, so be prepared to wait a while for a dip beneath the falls. ❸ 3 km (almost 2 miles) east of town off Carretera Jarabacoa ● Open daily 08.30–19.00 ❶ Admission charge

Salto Baiguate This waterfall has an impressive cave beneath its falls, and a larger swimming area for visitors. ❸ Just south of Jarabacoa on Carretera Constanza ● Open daily 08.30–19.00 ❶ Admission free

ADVENTURE TOURS
Iguana Mama ★★★
This team is a nationally recognized group of naturalists and guides that offer hiking excursions as well as mountain bike rentals and tours, canyoning and rafting trips and horse riding. ❸ Calle Principal 74, Cabarete ❶ 809 571 0908/0228 Ⓦ www.iguanamama.com

Rancho Baiguate ★★★
An environmentally responsible, full-service facility that offers lessons and tours for rafting, canyoning, rock wall climbing, parasailing, Pico Duarte hikes, bicycle tours of the area's waterfalls and more. Rafting tours require a minimum age of 12, although no experience is necessary. ❸ Carretera Constanza ❶ 809 574 4940 ❶ 809 574 6890 Ⓦ www.ranchobaiguate.com

Pico Duarte
a strenous but rewarding hike

Pico Duarte in the Cordillera Central is the Caribbean's tallest mountain, at a height of 3087 m (10,128 ft). The area around the mountain is largely uninhabited due to the lack of fresh water and its first recorded ascent was not until 1944, to celebrate the 100th anniversary of Dominican independence. Public trails were not even established here until the mid-1980s. However, today, around 3000 people climb it to admire the spectacular views from the top.

Those planning a hike should be aware that the high elevation is much cooler than other parts of the island, so extra clothing and rain gear are advised. Guides are also highly recommended and are a must if you are planning on camping overnight to reach the peak. The climb itself is quite a workout, even for experienced hikers, due to the trail's uneven quality – compacted dirt gives way to loose rock and requires sturdy ankles and proper hiking boots.

Within the park and during your hike you will see many birds unique to this region, including the palm chat, which is the country's national bird. Among other birds are the red-tailed hawk, the Hispañiolan parrot and the Zumbador hummingbird. Underfoot will appear several dozen different types of amphibians. Not native to the island, wild boar roam

HIKING ESSENTIALS
Backpack Matches or lighter, lighter fluid, food and utensils, bottled water and/or water purifier.
Rain or shine Waterproof (broken-in) hiking boots and hiking socks, waterproof sleeping bag, waterproof tent, waterproof jacket, hat and gloves, rain poncho, swimsuit.
Day pack Flashlight, first aid kit, insect repellent, sunblock, sunglasses, lip balm, toilet paper, (camera and film), binoculars.

the mountainsides along with other smaller mammals, including rodents. A wide assortment of trees includes mountain wild olive, West Indian laurel cherry, wild braziletto, and Creole pine. Naturalists will also be thrilled to see the source of the Yaque del Norte River.

Mountain trails are accessible from adjoining parks **Armando Bermúdez** and **José del Carmen Ramírez**, open 09.00–17.00 daily. Purchase the required access permit from ranger stations for a fee.

ADVENTURE TOURS

Iguana Mama This team's guided hikes up Pico Duarte are regarded as some of the region's best. Hikes span three days and two nights, and include dinner with a Dominican family (see page 77 for further details).

Rancho Baiguate Offers three-, four- and five-day hiking excursions to the top of Pico Duarte. The longer trip includes a hike through the Tetero Valley (see page 77 for further details).

◓ *Fantastic views can be had from Pico Duarte*

Parqué Nacional los Haitises
lush green hills and mangroves

Located on the south coast of the Samaná Peninsula, this national park of 208 sq km (80 sq miles) is home to many historical and natural sites and is one of the most visited parks in the country. Nearly 100 plant species can be found here, including bamboo, mangrove, mahogany and cedar. Over one hundred different bird species reside in the protected area, as well as the endangered solendon, a rodent which can be found in the extensive mangrove swamps that cover the bulk of the park.

Within the park are limestone caves once used by the Taino natives of the island, which still feature Taino faces carved directly into the walls. The standard two-and-a-half-hour boat tour brings visitors past the major points of interest in the park, which mostly consist of the Taino caves. One group of Taino caves, Cueva Arena, is a popular spot to start out. Here, many boats stop and allow passengers ashore to take pictures and experience the wonder of these grottoes, with drawings depicting images of daily life and local water creatures. Other caves in the area were hideout spots for infamous pirates, which adds some excitement to the place. As the boat moves on, the San Gabriel and Remington caves are often visited for their well-known Taino portraits – line drawings of faces on the cave walls. For bird enthusiasts, this is an opportunity to see pelicans, roseate terns, egrets and parakeets in the wild.

GETTING AROUND THE PARK
Visitors are only allowed into certain areas of the park due to its highly protected status, and these places can be visited by guided tour only. You can visit the park on foot but there are not many trails cut through and its swampy terrain makes it difficult to pass at best – the easiest way to get around is by boat. Many of the caves that you would want to view are located on the coast, and tours will bring you directly into the swamps, where you will be able to see the wildlife and the amazing

⬥ The Parqué Nacional los Haitises is a great place to explore

drawings up close.

There are two ways to tour the park by boat. You can take a ferry from Samaná (the landing is located on the Malecón across from the Banco Popular) to the town of **Sabana de la Mar**, where there is a choice of any number of *buscones* who will approach tourists for a group of two to four to ride out on a small boat for a one- to two-and-a-half-hour tour of the coast. Expect to pay extra for a guide to explain what you are seeing, and save a small amount for your park entrance fee.

The alternative is to book an excursion with a tour operator in **Samaná**, where you can often get a package that includes a round-trip fare, guide and lunch.

BOAT TOUR OPERATORS

Moto Marina Departing directly from Samaná, this excursion operator begins the tour in true Dominican style with a rum cocktail. Within a half hour, you are in the park and enjoying all it has to offer, with a fully trained guide. Snacks and lunch are served on the beach at the Taino caves, and guests have the option of stopping by Cayo Levantado for swimming before going back to home port. ❷ Avenida Malecón ❶ 809 538 2302 ❷ motomarina@yahoo.com

Victoria Marine Two departure points are offered with this tour, which includes guide, transportation and lunch. ❶ 809 538 2494 ❸ Malecón ❶ Two tours daily, departing at 09.00 and 13.30 ❸ Cayo Levantado ❶ Two tours daily, departing at 09.30 and 14.00

MS Tours SA Offering full-service, round-trip tours with guides directly from Samaná. ❸ Avenida Malecón 7 ❶ 809 538 2499/729 7993 ❷ ms_tours@hotmail.com

Parqué Nacional del Este & Isla Saona
history and nature in one

This national park, located in the extreme south-east of the country, contains some of the most extraordinary wildlife and historical sites on the island, and includes Isla Saona, a beautiful island off the southern coast. The park itself is suited for hiking and boating, and is not accessible to tourists in vehicles. These coastal regions are a magnificent place to see several endangered species, including the West Indian manatee, sea turtles and bottlenose dolphins, as well as rhinocerous, iguana and hutia. The park is also home to several Taino sites of historical importance.

A birdwatcher's paradise, this densely forested area is home to 112 known species. Several of these are unique to the island, such as the white-headed dove and the Hispañiolan lizard cuckoo. Offshore, surrounding waters are a good place to look for migrating humpback whales during

⬇ *Parqué Nacional del Este is a haven for many endangered species*

January and February, and to view the West Indian manatee, a large, grey aquatic mammal – its nearest land relative is the elephant.

ISLA SAONA

Visitors to this small island will find it populated with plenty of birds, but beware – there are nearly as many tacky tourist joints. This once-pristine island, although technically protected by national park status, has fallen victim to over-use, knocking the marine ecosystem out of balance due in part to over-fishing and illegal hunting, which has contributed to the extinction of vertebrates such as the Caribbean monk seal. The Nature Conservancy is now working with the Dominican Republic in an effort to re-establish this balance and save the fragile coral reefs that have been partially destroyed by just a couple of decades of careless snorkelling. It is still a beautiful place to visit, however, with some of the most picturesque beaches and palm forests imaginable.

Caves within the park are the main sites containing artefacts from Taino times, primarily **Cueva Jose Maria**, **Cueva del Puente**, and a more obscure site near **Penon Gordo** which requires a guide. The most fascinating objects are petroglyphs and pictographs depicting some of the first encounters between the native tribes and the Spanish invaders. All of these areas require a great deal of hiking – be well equipped with insect repellent, sunscreen and a good amount of fresh water.

It is easiest to visit the park on an organized tour. However, if not, you must pay the entrance fee at the national park office (ⓐ Playa Bayahibe ❶ 809 833 0022 ⏰ Open daily 08.30–12.30) and hire a park ranger as a guide, which is an additional charge. Some hire a private boat to motor around the coastal waters of the park, but if you plan on setting foot on park territory, you must have a guide.

TOUR OPERATORS FOR THE PARK
Casa Daniel Includes passage and lunch with guide. ⓐ Calle Principe 1, Playa Bayahibe ❶ 809 833 0050
ScubaFun Boat tour with meal included. ⓐ Calle Principe 28, Playa Bayahibe ❶ 809 833 0003

Lago Enriquillo & Isla Cabritos
a vast and lovely saltwater lake

Sitting between Sierra de Neiba to the north and Sierra Barohuch to the south is the valley that is home to Lago Enriquillo and the Isla Cabritos National Park. This area has been a national park for decades, protecting not only the lowest point in the Caribbean – 44 m (144 ft) below sea level – but also many endangered species and several places of historical interest. The park consists of the island it is named for as well as Lake Enriquillo and its surrounding shores.

Lake Enriquillo was at one time a channel that connected Port-Au-Prince and the Bahía de Neiba, which was stranded inland when the earth's continental plates shifted. The result was a saltwater lake, which is constantly fed by rivers flowing from the surrounding mountains. It sits only 42 km (26 miles) from the border of Haiti.

Having once been completely under water, the shores of the lake still contain pieces of coral from prehistoric times. Living in the rivers that feed the lake is an abundance of American crocodiles, most readily found in the Rio de Descubierta and avoiding the salt water. This river is a favourite place for flamingos to flock, and you will probably be able to spot a heron here.

The lake was named after the Taino chief Enriquillo, who resisted the Spaniards for nearly 15 years by hiding out in the surrounding caves. He and his followers held out long enough to eventually achieve a peace treaty with the Spaniards, but unfortunately Enriquillo died of smallpox soon afterward. He is commemorated by a statue along Route 46.

ISLA CABRITOS

The Isla Cabritos National Park is on the largest of three islands found in the center of Lake Enriquillo, the other two being the smaller and rarely visited islands of Barbarita and Islita. Isla Cabritos, which translates to 'Little Goats' Island', sits 4–40 m (13–130 ft) below sea

level in Lake Enriquillo, and was at one time completely under water. It is 12 km (7¹/₂ miles) long and is mostly a flat, desert habitat. It receives less than 50 cm (20 inches) of rainfall each year and temperatures sometimes climb to 44°C (112°F). The landscape is peppered with cacti and is home to an astounding number of reptiles, including the endangered rhinoceros iguana and Ricord iguana. Many of the iguanas on the island are over 20 years old and as large and tame as housecats, accustomed to the frequent visitors that often stop by with less-than-healthy snacks. The island is also home to a number of birds, including the West Indian nighthawk and the burrowing owl.

Those interested in Taino art will want to visit **Las Caritas** ('the little faces'), which is located near the park entrance on the highway. If you are up for a rocky climb, you can get up close to these petroglyphs that are visible from the road below, which are actually carved into petrified coral, not rock. Many believe that these mark a special ceremonial site, although little is known about them.

TOURS IN THE PARK

Tours are conducted by boat and can last from one to two-and-a-half hours, so bring plenty of fresh water and sunscreen. Isla Cabritos is less intense, and is good for viewing large iguanas, which are friendly to tourists. Morning tours are the best for viewing wildlife, especially crocodiles, and the most comfortable for passengers. Guides are not usually very talkative nor informative, but the scenery should be sufficient to keep you well occupied. Most tours stop on the island for a walk about. Visitor information is available from the Division of National Parks (ⓐ Calle Damas 6, Old City, Santo Domingo ⓣ 809 685 1316).

The entrance to Lago Enriquillo and Isla Cabritos park area is marked by a bright yellow and green sign, 3 km (almost 2 miles) east of La Descubierta along Highway 46. ⓒ Open daily 07.00–17.00 ⓘ Admission charge

Discovering amber
one of the world's most unique gemstones

Amber is one of the Dominican Republic's best-known products, and if you admire this unusual gemstone, it can provide the theme for several interesting places to visit, from jewellery shops, galleries and museums to a hiking excursion to the mines themselves.

Unlike most gemstones, which are mineral in origin, amber is formed when resin that has seeped out of trees is fossilized. What makes amber even more fascinating is that prehistoric insects, plants, spiders, feathers and even the occasional lizard or frog can be found trapped inside it. Don't expect to find any examples of the latter for sale, however – they are very rare.

Dominican amber is especially clear and has a higher incidence of trapped insects, making it some of the most sought-after in the world. Although most amber is in shades of yellow and brown, it is sometimes found in red, rarely in a dusty green colour and – only in the Dominican Republic – in blue. Dominican amber is about 25 million years old, and the insects and plants it contains have been extinct for many millions of years – so has the species of tree that formed the resin.

Most of the Dominican Republic's amber comes from two areas; in the mountains north of the city of Santiago and around the towns of El Valle and Cotui, north-east of Santo Domingo. A small amount comes from the Bayaguana area, in the east near Sabana, but it is younger – a mere 15–17 million years old.

The best quality – the oldest and the hardest – is that from the La Cumbre region, in the central Cordillera Septentrional mountain range between Puerto Plata and Santiago. The La Toca, Palo Quemado, La Bucara, and Los Cacaos mines are in this region, revealing amber that is 33–40 million years old. Slightly younger – about 25 million years old – is the amber found in the Palo Alto area, also near Santiago. The Los Cacaos mines are the source of the very rare blue amber.

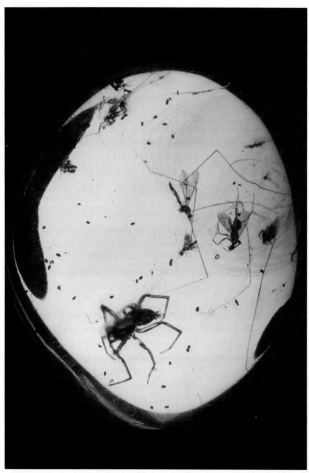

⬤ *Discover the many shades of Dominican amber*

THINGS TO SEE & DO

Galleria de Ambar ★

Although it includes more Dominican products than amber and has a strong shopping component, Galleria de Ambar does have interesting exhibits, as well as signage in English. ❸ Calle 12 de Julio, Puerto Plata ❶ 809 586 6467 ❿ www.ambercollection.itgo.com ❶ Open Mon–Fri 08.30–18.00 and Sat 09.00–13.00

Museo de Ambar (Amber Museum) ★★

The island's best and most complete amber museum is the life work of a Dominican family, located in this gracious old mansion. The collections,

FAKE OR REAL?

To the untrained eye, a fly or a bit of dried flower that was encased in orange-coloured plastic a week ago can look very convincingly like a piece of amber millions of years old. To complicate matters, copal – unfossilized resin of a much younger age – can also contain insects and plants, and has a similar colour. How can you be sure what you're getting is real amber? Here are some tips from the experts:

Know the source If you shop at a museum shop or a well-known and reputable jeweller, you can be sure of getting the real thing – and in top quality.

Rub the stone vigorously The ancient Greek name for amber – *electron* – is the basis for our word electricity. The Greeks first noticed that if you rub amber repeatedly on a piece of cotton cloth, it will generate static electricity that will attract hair or other light natural substance. Neither plastic nor copal will do this.

Look at it under fluorescent light If the stone glows with a changed colour, it is real. Reputable dealers will have fluorescent lamps available so that you can perform this simple test and confirm that you are spending money on the real thing.

begun in 1970, are not only varied, but contain some of the world's rarest examples of amber – including an amber-encased lizard – one of fewer than two dozen ever found. Flowers, insects and mosses are also to be found, preserved as if yesterday, inside the specimens. 📍 Villa Berzt, Calle Duarte and Castellanos, Puerto Plata ☎ 809 586 2848 🌐 www.ambermuseum.com 🕐 Open Mon–Sat 09.00–18.00, closed Sun ℹ Admission charge

Museo de Historia Natural (Natural History Museum) ★★

Geology forms a major part of this museum, which helps put amber into the larger picture of the island's formation. Learn how other fossils were formed, as well as the natural history of amber. If you have children with you, there is plenty here to keep them occupied while you learn about amber. 📍 Plaza de la Cultura, Santo Domingo ☎ 809 689 0106 🕐 Open Tues–Sun 10.00–17.00, closed Mon ℹ Admission charge

Museo Mundo de Ambar (Amber World Museum) ★

This museum's informative displays of Dominican amber include examples in several colours, as well as a wide variety of flora and fauna embedded in the stones. In the workshop you can see raw amber being polished and set into jewellery, which you can buy in the museum shop. 📍 Arz. Merino 452 (Zona Colonial), Santo Domingo ☎ 809 682 3309 🌐 www.amberworldmuseum.com 🕐 Open daily 09.00–18.00

Visiting amber mines ★

The most easily visited amber mines are those in the mountains between Puerto Plata and Santiago. The mines are near the crest of the mountains, where the amber lies between layers of sandstone that has been uplifted. Often these veins are discovered when a landslide exposes a strata of black lignite among the lighter sandstone. This is where the pieces of amber will be found. Depending on the angle of these layers, pits are dug into the mountain or into the cliffs. The amber is painstakingly carved out by hand, with chisels and machetes.

It is important to arrive at the mines with a realistic view of what to expect. For example, hoping to see any semblance of elaborate mining operations will prove disappointing. The sites are scattered and usually consist of a hole or shaft, roughly supported by a few logs. Workmen burn candles – this warns them of decreased oxygen in the air – and the only 'building' is likely to be a shelter of tarpaulin on sticks, weighted down by stones. Also important to note is that these mines are in remote places, accessible only on foot. They are not on everyone's agenda!

Although no regularly scheduled tours go to the mines from the resorts, it is possible to arrange one if you ask around, especially at the **Museo del Ambar** in Puerto Plata (see page 89). Or contact **Tours Trips Treks & Travel** (❶ 809 867 8884/270 8390 (mobile) ❶ 206 600 1700 ⓦ www.4Tdomrep.com).

SHOPPING FOR AMBER

Raw amber is usually polished to bring out its lustre and to show off the insects or plant life encased in it. Some of the shops have craftsmen working there, so you can see this process. Another unusual gem called larimar, a semi-precious turquoise blue stone found only in the Dominican Republic, is often sold in the same shops as amber.

Ambar Tres ❸ La Atarazana 3, Zona Colonial, Santo Domingo ❶ 809 688 0474

Museo Larimar Dominicano ❸ Isabela la Catolica, Santo Domingo ❶ 809 689 6605 ❷ Open daily 09.00–18.00

The Amber Factory ❸ Arz. Merino 452, Zona Colonial, Santo Domingo ❶ 809 686 5700 ⓦ www.amberfactory.com

Museo de Ambar Dominicano Gift Shop ❸ Duarte 61, Puerto Plata ❶ 809 586 3910 ❷ Open Mon–Sat 09.00–18.00

Amber Shop ❸ Playa Dorada Plaza, Puerto Plata ❶ 809 209 2215 ❷ Open Mon–Sat 09.00–18.00

Patrick's Silversmithy ❸ Pedro Clisante 9, Sosúa ❶ 809 571 2121

Diving excursions
underwater thrills

For many underwater lovers, diving is what the Dominican Republic is all about. The extraordinary reefs and waters surrounding its beautiful beaches are filled with colourful sea life, and diving services offer equipment and lessons.

EAST OF SANTO DOMINGO

Parque Nacional Submarino La Caleta, about 35 km (22 miles) east of the capital, is a coral-reef in process around the scuttled treasure hunt ship *The Hickory*. Reaching to 180 m (590 ft), the protected area is perfect for divers who want to explore the open hull and the tropical sea life that frequents it. There is no official diving service setup, so make arrangements with your resort or with a diving service nearby.

Scuba Caribe SA This outfit offers diving services in five different locations in Punta Caña, with lessons and rentals for beginners through to experienced scuba divers. ⓐ Carretera Friusa 1 ❶ 809 221 1336/809 552 0379

SAMANÁ PENINSULA

The best dive sites in this area are **Dive The Tower**, a mountain rising from the sea, with a 50 m (165 ft) submerged mountainside alive with brilliant sea life, and **La Catedral**, a huge, underwater cave that has formed an air pocket. For advanced divers, **Plaza Monica** is a reef 30 m (100 ft) down, with a large population of sea life. At **Cabo Cabron**, divers may even hear the songs of migrating whales.

Dive Samaná A company that provides rentals and transportation to diving locations in the area. ⓐ Casa Marina Bay Resort ❶ 809 538 0210 ❶ Open daily

Stellina Dive Centre This place makes dive trips by advance reservation to both the popular and little-known sites. ⓐ Hotel Cacao Beach, Las Terrenas ⓣ 809 240 6000

AMBER COAST

The dive capital of this north coast is **Sosúa**, where there are dozens of sites, in all skill levels. Reefs swim with spectacular fish, and are easy to reach. Most of these are multi-faceted reefs, with plenty of opportunities for beginners but enough depth to satisfy experts as well.

⬥ *Many visitors come to the Dominican Republic for the underwater scenery*

The sunken cargo ship *Zingara* lies 36 m (118 ft) below the surface, with a shallow reef wall above which novice divers can enjoy the fan corals and tube sponges. Experienced divers should aim for **Paradise Reef**, which also has something for everyone, with a bright coral reef at about 12 m (39 ft), and octopus and squid at 32 m (105 ft). **Garden of Los Charamicaos** has large sponges and bright fan corals at a maximum depth of 24 m (79 ft). **Pyramids** was formed by erosion, with corals at 15 m (49 ft) down. One of the best spots is **Airport Wall**, a 24 m (79 ft) area with several caves and some elkhorn coral.

Soficap This company offers diving equipment rentals and instruction for the Cabarete beach area. ❸ Carretera Cabarete ❶ 809 571 0280 ❶ Open daily, by appointment

Hippocampo Dive Centre This centre has individual and group diving classes for beginners and brush-up courses for those who have not dived recently. A good selection of rentals and equipment for sale make this a full-service dive shop. ❸ Carretera Cabarete ❶ 809 571 0834

Gri-Gri Divers A wide variety of packages for all levels is available here, and trips are offered to 13 different nearby dive sites. The fully-certified staff is multilingual. ❸ Rio San Juan ❶ 809 589 2671

> **SAFETY FIRST**
> Most resorts offer diving services or can put you in touch with a reliable guide. This is much safer than making independent plans with the local fishermen, since the professional dive boats are equipped with proper safety devices and are operated by trained divers.

Food & drink

The traditional foods of the Dominican people are a mixture of ancient recipes from Taino tribes and the influences of Spanish settlers and other European and African populations. Beans and rice are the staple food and chicken is the most popular meat, often found fried or roasted at informal eateries along the streets and beaches. Rum is by far the most well-known Dominican drink, but locals enjoy plenty of non-alcoholic fruit drinks as well, taking full advantage of their tropical treats.

SPECIALITIES
Casabe
Made from the yucca (also known as cassava), a large tuber native to the island of Hispaniola, this dish is made in almost exactly same way it was back in Taino times. The plant is hand-ground, pressed and flattened into discs and then baked into a tortilla-like sheet. These are very high in fibre and low in fat, and are eaten with meals or alone as a snack.

Pan de agua
A medium-length bread translated as, simply, 'water bread', it contains yeast and is another staple in the Dominican diet.

DESSERTS
Harina de maiz (corn meal pudding) Also served as a breakfast dish, this dish is prepared with evaporated milk and is a sweetened version of polenta, with cinnamon and nutmeg added. It can be served warm or cold.

Masitas (coconut biscuits) A simple cookie made from fresh coconut chunks, found throughout the country.

Flan (caramel cream pudding) Brought to the island by the Spanish, this thick, corn-based custard made with egg yolks and heavy cream is a particular favourite of Dominicans.

Jalea de batata (sweet potato pudding) A very sweet delicacy prepared with shredded coconut, milk, butter, cloves and cinnamon.

MEAL TIMES
Breakfast

If you have a sensitive stomach, plan to stay in for the continental spread at your hotel – Dominican breakfasts are traditionally hearty and rich, designed for farmworkers preparing for a long day in the fields. It is not unusual to see a local restaurant serving deep-fried salami and cheese to accompany fried eggs and onions with ham. To expand on the food groups, there may be a few slices of boiled yucca, and certainly a freshly roasted and brewed cup of sweet coffee with milk.

Dinner (lunch)

Served during the time that most western countries refer to as lunch, this large meal precedes siesta. Lasting an average of at least an hour and possibly more, it features a hearty meat course with a vegetable such as green beans, as well as a starch such as sweet potato or rice. Favourite meat dishes include *rabo encendido*, which is a spicy soup made from oxtails, or *asopao*, a general name for a rice-based soup that may have seafood, chicken, pork or beef and an assortment of spices.

Supper

The final meal of the day, supper is often served late in the evening after the air has cooled and the family has had a chance to return home. Traditionally it is the meal when the family gets together, and the focus is less on eating and more on socializing. Typical dishes at the late meal are chicken based, such as *pica pollo*, which is breaded fried chicken.

FRUITS

Here you can find many of the exotic fruits that are rare and expensive at home, so fill up on guava smoothies, chilled passionfruit, or the Dominican favourite, *morir soñado*, which includes fresh orange juice, sugar and milk

🔺 *Dominican rum is used to create many exotic cocktails*

blended together. Bananas, guava and star fruit are just a few of the
other options for a fresh drink or fruit salad, and everyone should try
fresh coconut milk before leaving the island.

BEVERAGES
Rum
Of the Dominican rums, Bermúdez is considered the best. The quality to look for in buying your rum is its colour (the darker, the better) and its age. Barceló and Brugal brands are also considered top quality, but there are many private labels that your concierge or a local merchant may recommend that should not be overlooked. If you want your rum to last the evening, order a *cuba libre servicio* and you will get a bottle of rum, two cokes and a bucket of ice. Check that the ice was not frozen from the local tap water before you drink, though.

Mabì
Mabì has a rather low alcohol content compared to rum, and is made with the native plant, *behuco de indio*. The processed vine is mixed with brown sugar and water and fermented in the sun for three days, resulting in a cider-like drink.

Beer & wine
There are plenty of beers to choose between. Most popular is the island's Presidente, which comes in a bottle that might be much larger than you are used to, so be sure to work up a thirst before ordering.

Dominican wines are perhaps worth a sip for the experience, but do not go searching too far – the country is not well known for its fine national vintages and imported wines are expensive. If you are looking for a genuine wine drink of the locals, seek out *mama juana*, a concoction of wine, rum, honey and plants, which is fermented both underground and in the sun to create supposed aphrodisiac qualities.

Non-alcoholic beverages
In addition to a plethora of fruit juices that can be served alone (see pages 97–98), mixed or blended with ice, the Dominican Republic is well known as a coffee producer. In fact, some of the finest coffees in the world are grown and roasted here; locals enjoy it as an after-meal beverage with sugar and with or without milk.

Menu decoder

MEALS & BEVERAGES

asopao Thick soup made with rice and seafood or meat

bandera dominicana Typical Dominican lunch of rice, beans and meat

casabe Cassava bread, thick tortilla made with dried yucca

chicharron Fried pork rind

cocido Meaty stew

fría A very cold beer (literally means 'cold')

locrio A combination of rice, meat (maybe seafood) and vegetables

longaniza Spicy pork sausage

mabi Cider-like alcoholic beverage

mangú Mashed plantains, yucca, and yautía

moro Traditional dish made with rice and beans

pica pollo Breaded fried chicken

puerco en puya Pork roasted on a spit

rabo encendido Spicy oxtail soup

rés guisada Beef stew

sancocho A Dominican stew made with up to seven types of meat

COMMON TERMS

al ajillo In garlic sauce

al horno Roasted with lemon

al oregano With heavy cream and oregano sauce

con coco With coconut milk, tomato, and garlic sauce

criolla With spicy, tomato-based sauce

mariscos Seafood

picadera Buffet or appetizers

picante Spicy hot

pincho Brochette/kebab

salsa de tomate Tomato paste

COMMON INGREDIENTS

arroz Rice

aguacate Avocado

auyama Gem squash (also known as calabaza)

bacalao Codfish

batata Sweet potato (also known as camote and boniato)

bija anato, **annato** or **achiote** Red seeds used to color foods

china Orange

chivo Goat

cilantro Coriander

garbanzos Chick peas

guayaba Guava

guineo Banana

habas Fava beans

habichuelas pintas Pinta beans

lambí Conch

langosta Clawless lobster

leche Milk

lechoza pawpaw Usually known as papaya (or simply pawpaw)

limoncillo Spanish lemon

maní Peanuts (also known as cacahuate or cacahuete)

mondongo Tripe (also known as panza, tripas or menudos)

naranja Orange

nuez moscada Nutmeg

papa Potato

platano Plantain

pulpo Octopus

remolacha Beet

salsa inglesa Worcestershire sauce

vainitas Green beans

yucca Cassava, root of the yucca plant, also known as mandioca

Shopping

There are a couple of important things to remember when shopping in the Dominican Republic. Firstly, pickpockets target tourists, so conceal your money and important papers well, and do not carry large amounts of money on you or take out large sums from ATMs. Secondly, haggling for your price is expected in most settings.

MARKETS
To find authentic local markets, which are usually held every day in large cities and less frequently in smaller towns, it is best to ask your host or any local to point you in the right direction.

AMBER & LARIMAR
Ambar Tres ⓐ La Atarazana 3, Zona Colonial, Santo Domingo ⓣ 809 688 0474

Museo Larimar Dominicano ⓐ Isabela la Catolica, Santo Domingo ⓣ 809 689 6605 ⓛ Open daily 09.00–18.00

Museo del Ambar Dominicano Gift Shop ⓐ Duarte 61, Puerto Plata ⓣ 809 586 3910 ⓛ Open Mon–Sat 09.00–18.00, closed Sun

CIGARS & TOBACCO
Cigar King ⓐ El Conde 458, Santo Domingo ⓣ 809 689 2565 ⓛ Open Mon–Sat 09.30–noon and 15.00–17.30, closed Sun

Renaissance Jaragua Hotel & Casino ⓐ Avenida George Washington 367 (El Malecón), Santo Domingo ⓣ 809 221 1483

Cuevas y Hermanos Fabricantes de cigarros ⓐ Avenida General López, Puerto Plata ⓣ 809 970 0903 ⓛ Open Tues–Sun 13.00–17.00 and 21.00–midnight, closed Mon

MAJOR SHOPPING CITIES
Santiago (page 66)
Calle del Sol The city's main shopping district, with large stores, sidewalk vendors, banks and other services.

La Romana (page 32)
Altos de Chavon This top-end shopping complex has a wide range of shops as well as plenty of very good restaurants that often feature evening entertainment.

Santo Domingo (page 14)
El Mercado Modelo A sheltered market specializing in authentic native crafts. ⓐ Calle Mella, Zona Colonial

⬢ *Colourful local artworks for sale*

Calle El Conde Reasonably priced shopping district with trendy shops. ⓐ Zona Colonial

Plaza Central Home to several international brand-name boutiques. ⓐ Avenidas Winston Churchill and Avenida 27 de Febrero

Sosúa (page 53)
Taimascaros Contains an astonishing collection of carnival art including masks and costumes. ⓐ Camino Libre 70 ⓣ 809 571 3138

Puerto Plata (page 58)
Mercado Nuevo Large souvenir market renowned for good, old-fashioned haggling. ⓐ Off El Morro between Villa Nueva and Avenida José Ramon Lopez

Kids

Dominicans love children and they are welcome in all but the most expensive restaurants, expecially in the resort towns. The resorts have plenty of activities on offer and often have good childcare facilities too.

FUN ATTRACTIONS & WATER PARKS

Agua Splash ★★

A typical water park with waterslides and pools (see page 15). ➋ Avenida Espana, Santo Domingo ➊ 809 591 5927 ➌ Open Tues–Sun 10.30–17.00

Columbus Aquaparque ★

Equipped with shops, restaurants, and bars to keep the land-lubbers content (see page 55). ➋ Carretera Sosúa Plata, Sosúa ➊ 809 571 2642/2254 ➌ Open daily 10.00–18.00

FunCity Action Park ★★

Go-carts, bumper cars, grand prix and more, plus a special kiddie section for ages 2-8, with food and beverages on site (see page 55). ➌ Carretera Puerto Plata, Km 5, Sosúa ➊ 809 320 1031 ➍ www.funcity-gocarts.com ➌ Open daily ➊ Admission charge; shuttle services to and from Sosúa and other nearby towns provided

Parque Zoológico Nacional (National Zoo) ★★★

Kids will love the crocodiles, hyenas, and other wild beasts here (see page 18). ➋ Paseo de los Reyes Catolicos and Avedida José Ortega y Gassett, Santo Domingo ➊ 809 563 3149 ➌ Open Mon–Fri 09.00–17.00, Sat–Sun 09.00–17.30 ➊ Admission charge

Rancho Cumayasa Eco ★★

This resort is home to the popular children's attraction 'Hurricane House' (see page 34). ➌ Highway 4, La Romana ➊ 809 757 0535 ➊ Non-guests need to buy a day pass, which includes lunch, a one-hour horse ride, and access to the paddleboats and other facilities.

Ocean World ★★
Swimming with sharks, dolphins, sea lions, and more (see page 63).
ⓐ Ppal 2 Cofresí, Puerto Plata ⓣ 809 291 1111 ⓦ www.ocean-world.info
ⓒ Open daily

WHALE WATCHING
Whale Samaná & Victoria Marine, Samaná Two departure points are
offered: **Malecón** (ⓣ 809 538 2494 ⓒ Two tours daily, at 09.00 and 13.30) and
Cavo Levantado (ⓒ Two tours daily, at 09.30 and 14.00 ⓒ Open Jan–Mar).

Moto Marina Whale watching tours. ⓐ Avenida Malecón No. 3, Samaná
ⓣ 809 538 2302 ⓔ motomarina@yahoo.com ⓒ Open Jan–Mar

Don't forget the importance of waterproof sunscreen – preferably
SPF35 or higher. Be sure there is a lifeguard on duty before your
children swim in the ocean, because the currents are unpredictable.
Make sure they drink plenty of water; children (as well as adults) should
always drink bottled water and also use it for brushing their teeth.

● *Swimming with dolphins at Ocean World*

Sports & activities

BASEBALL

No other sport takes hold of the Dominican republic like *béisbol*; it is an unofficial national religion. Currently there are over 400 Dominican players in the US Major Leagues (for more details on Dominican players, see ⓦ www.baseball-reference.com). The season runs October– January but is played year-round by kids in the streets or adults in the country's various stadiums. Tickets are usually sold-out well in advance, but there are always 'scalpers' or touts selling tickets outside the stadiums. Check also with your hotel concierge or taxi driver as you never know what connections they might have and it could be much cheaper for you.

Baseball Stadiums

Estadio Quisqueya ❸ Avenida Tiradentes, Santo Domingo ❶ 809 540 5772 ⓛ Game times vary ❶ Admission charge

Estadio Tetelo Vargas (Tetelo Vargas Stadium) ❸ Avenida Circunvalacion and Carretera Mella ❶ Admission charge

Online baseball and event tickets ⓦ www.ticketexpress.com

COCKFIGHTING

This tradition is a highly controversial, but deeply ingrained part of Dominican culture. Weekends are cockfighting days in almost every town and city in the country. These events are accompanied by an almost carnivalesque atmosphere of drinking, betting and yelling. Be aware that cockfighting is bloody and puts the animals through a lot of pain. ❸ In Santo Domingo, fights take place at the Coliseo Galístico de Santo Domingo on Avenida Luperón

GOLF

There are plenty of golf courses in the Dominican Republic. Most are to be found along the coast in the country's burgeoning resorts. The three best are at Casa de Campo in La Romana, Playa Dorada and Playa Grande. The latter two are the most reasonable, but green fees at the Teeth of the Dog course at Casa de Campo will cost you a hefty sum.

WATER SPORTS

Water lovers will find no shortage of activities on offer at any of the resorts on the island. Try your hand at windsurfing, snorkelling, parasailing, sailing, deep sea fishing and more. Cabarete (see pages 46–52) is considered one of the finest windsurfing locations in the world and scuba diving and kiteboarding are also on offer. Whether you're an experienced diver or a beginner, exploring the spectacular array of colourful marine life and shipwrecks in the incredibly clear Caribbean waters is a must. See 'Diving excursions' pages 92–94 for more details. For snorkelling, the beach at La Isabela on the north coast, though best known for its Columbus connection (see page 63), also boasts an incredible array of underwater life.

⬤ *Explore the waters by sailboat*

Festivals & events

CARNIVAL

Celebrated every Sunday in February and ending in a huge event at the end of the month right before Lent, Carnival is an exciting time all over the island. The cities of La Vega, Santiago, Monte Cristi, and Santo Domingo hold the most boisterous and well known celebrations nation-wide, drawing in crowds from all over the world. Residents spend the entire year working on their costumes, which are often a work of art. Masks depicting *el Diablo* (the devil) are very common, as well as bright and festive dresses. If you are planning on watching a parade, beware of the more violent traditions, including flailing whips and heavy balloons.

MERENGUE FESTIVAL

In July and August each year, Santo Domingo is host to an enormous merengue festival where the best of the best dancers perform all over the city. It is hard to miss the excitement, even if you try!

Early October is Puerto Plata's annual merengue festival, located on its Malecón (promenade). For the festivities, the area is converted into a fairgrounds of sorts, with only foot traffic allowed and local crafts and foods for sale.

LATIN MUSIC FESTIVAL

Held at the Olympic Stadium in Santo Domingo each year in October, the Latin Music Festival attracts internationally known Latin musicians who showcase and celebrate the art form, spanning the genres of salsa, merengue, bachata, and jazz.

CREOLE MUSIC FESTIVAL

This festival, held the last weekend in October each year, is the newest festival on the island, having run for only the past nine years or so. It features some of the most renowned musical groups and soloists from the Creole-speaking world. Musical forms include calypso, soukous and zydeco (from the US state of Louisiana).

⬧ *Participants wear flamboyant costumes for the Santo Domingo Carnival*

NATIONAL & CULTURAL HOLIDAYS AT A GLANCE

1 January	New Year's Day
6 January	Three King's Day / Epiphany
21 January	Our Lady of Altagracia
26 January	Duarte Day
27 February	Independence Day
March/April (week before Easter)	Semana Santa
14 April	Pan American Day
1 May	Labour Day
10 June	Feast of Corpus Christi
16 July	Foundation of Sociedad la Trinitaria
16 August	Restoration Day
24 September	Our Lady of Mercedes
12 October	Columbus Day
24 October	UN Day
1 November	All Saint's Day
6 November	Constitution Day
25 December	Christmas Day

TRAVELLING DURING NATIONAL HOLIDAYS

You may find that banks, government offices, museums, and some shops are closed on these days. There are also often parades and other festivities that may block off roads or several city blocks and deter plans on the short term. It is always wise to ask your host for advice before travelling on your own during these times. **Semana Santa**, the week before Easter, is the time during which you will most likely be inconvenienced by the holiday status. Strangely enough, although water sports are prohibited during this time, this is when you will find beaches and pools at their most crowded, as well as hotels and just about everywhere else.

Preparing to go

GETTING THERE

The least expensive way to get to the Dominican Republic is to book a package holiday with one of the various leading tour operators. Most companies offer deals that give the option of flight-only or combined flight and accommodation packages at very competitive prices compared to calling a resort directly. If you are flexible with your travel times and are not limited by school holidays, it is wise to take advantage of the last-minute deals offered by many of the popular websites. Weekend travel sections of your newspaper are also a likely place to find advertisements offering specials on airfare and lodging. The classified section may also prove useful in finding a private home or apartment to rent for your stay.

BEFORE YOU LEAVE

To ensure that your holiday is an enjoyable one, begin preparing well in advance to be sure everything is in order. It is a good idea to pack a small first-aid kit to carry with you, containing plasters, antiseptic cream, travel-sickness pills, insect repellent and/or bite-relief cream, antihistamine tablets, upset stomach remedies and painkillers, alcohol wipes (pre-packaged variety), condoms if you plan on being sexually active (AIDS is a health threat on this island), a pair of scissors or a folding knife (packed in check-through luggage), as well as sun lotion of SPF 35 or higher and after-sun cream. If you are taking prescription medicines, ensure that you take enough for the duration of your visit as you may not be able to buy them when you arrive. Pack in your carry-on luggage with an extra copy of the information sheet in case of loss. It is also worth having a dental check-up before you leave the UK.

DOCUMENTS

The most important documents you will need are your tickets and your passport. Check well in advance that your passport is up to date and has at least three months left to run (six months is even better). All children, including newborn babies, need their own passports now. It generally takes at least three weeks to process a passport renewal. This can be longer in the run-up to the summer months. Contact the **Passport Agency** for the latest information on how to renew your passport and the processing times involved. ☎ 0870 521 0410 ⊛ www.ukpa.gov.uk.

For the UK, each person (including children, even if they are travelling on their parents' passport), also requires a Tourist Card. They are available on arrival at the airport ($10 US at time of writing) or, in person or by post, in advance from the Dominican Embassy (see details below).

You should check the details of your travel tickets well before your departure, ensuring that the timings and dates are correct.

If you are thinking of hiring a car while you are away, you will need to have your UK driving licence with you. If you want more than one driver for the car, the other drivers must have their licences too.

Because of the increasing problem of international child abduction, anyone travelling with a child who has a different surname needs to have a certified letter certifying guardianship or an original or certified copy of the child's birth certificate on their person in case there is a need to prove the relationship. For more information on this, contact the **Dominican Embassy** ❸ 139 Inverness Terrace, Bayswater, W2-6JF, London ☎ 020 7727 6285 ☎ 020 7727 3693 ⊛ www.dominicanembassy.org.uk

MONEY

The currency is the peso (RD$). US dollars are also widely accepted, especially in the high-end resorts. The traditional way of carrying money, buying traveller's cheques and exchanging your currency for pesos and pesetas is becoming a thing of the past. The global economy is making

TELEPHONING THE DOMINICAN REPUBLIC

To telephone the Dominican Republic from the UK, first dial 00 1 then the national area code (809) followed by the seven-digit number.

the Euro, pound and dollar often freely traded currencies in markets, and credits cards are accepted by major shops, restaurants, hotels and even some tour operators. Cash machines (ATMs) line each shopping district, and it is actually much easier and safer to withdraw smaller amounts more frequently this way, rather than exchanging money, as long as you avoid those with high transaction fees.

When you need to exchange currency, look for a 'casa de cambio' instead of asking at your hotel or resort. The rates here or at a bank will be much better, sometimes double that which you would get otherwise. Never trust anyone who offers to exchange money on the street. Always be sure to ask for plenty of small notes (RD$20 or smaller) and some change, which is useful when trying to bargain in markets.

TRAVEL INSURANCE

Do you have sufficient cover for your holiday? Check that your policy covers you adequately for loss of possessions and valuables, for activities you might want to try – such as scuba diving, horse riding, or water sports – and for emergency medical and dental treatment, including flights home if required., and especially if you suffer from any chronic health conditions.

CLIMATE

The island's climate is generally warm – about 29°C (84°F) year-round. Waters along the Caribbean coast are temperate and perfect for swimming, and the Atlantic coast is just a bit cooler. Summer temperatures can rise up to 35°C (95°F), and can be stifling without air-conditioning. The mountain regions are far cooler, averaging a temperature of 24°C (75°F), and even below freezing at the top of Pico Duarte.

The rainy seasons here vary quite a bit by region, despite the country's small size. The Samaná Peninsula gets the most rain, with respite during the months of February and March. From May to October, expect Santo Domingo to get most of the daily downpour. The north coast has its turn come October, lasting as late as March. Fortunately, tropical rain storms come and go quickly, often cooling off a humid day instead of spoiling a holiday.

The rains that can hamper a holiday are hurricanes, which typically hit the island from August through October. The eastern side of the island is usually hit the hardest, with damage ranging from flooding to complete devastation. Despite increased hurricane activity during recent years, visitors continue to come during these months. If you are near the shore when a hurricane is approaching, try to get at least several kilometres inland, and head for one of the large resorts where the facilities are well prepared.

SECURITY

Take sensible precautions to prevent your house from being burgled while you are away:

- Cancel milk, newspapers, and other regular deliveries so that post and milk does not pile up, indicating that you are away.
- Let the postman know where to leave parcels and bulky mail that will not go through your letterbox – ideally with a next-door neighbour.
- If possible, arrange for a friend or neighbour to visit regularly, closing and opening curtains in the morning and evening, and switching lights on and off to give the impression that the house is being lived in.
- Consider buying electrical timing devices that will switch lights on and off, again to give the impression that there is someone in the house.
- Let Neighbourhood Watch representatives know that you will be away so that they can keep a watch on your home.
- If you have a burglar alarm, make sure that it is serviced and working properly and is switched on when you leave (you may find that your insurance policy requires this). Ensure that a neighbour is able to gain access to the alarm to turn it off if it is set off accidentally.
- If you are leaving cars unattended, put them in a garage, if possible, and leave a key with a neighbour in case the alarm goes off.

AIRPORT PARKING & ACCOMMODATION

If you intend to leave your car in an airport car park while you are away, or stay the night at an airport hotel before or after your flight, you should book well ahead to take advantage of discounts or cheap off-airport parking. Airport accommodation gets booked up several weeks in advance, especially during the height of the holiday season. Check whether the hotel offers free parking for the duration of the holiday – often the savings made on parking costs can significantly reduce the accommodation price.

BAGGAGE ALLOWANCES

Baggage allowances vary according to the airline, destination and the class of travel, but 20 kg (44 lb) per person is the norm for luggage that is carried in the hold. If in doubt, check your ticket – it usually tells you the weight limit. You are also allowed one item of cabin baggage weighing no more than 5 kg (11 lb) and measuring no larger than 46 by 30 by 23 cm (18 by 12 by 9 in). This restriction is more strictly enforced than it was in the past. Despite this limitation, it is a good idea to try and pack at least a day's change of clothes and anything of vital importance in your carry-on baggage in the event that the checked luggage is delayed upon arrival. Women are also allowed to carry handbags, and passengers are usually able to have their duty-free bags, umbrellas and coats held separately. It is a good idea to contact the airline ahead of time if you plan on bringing large or awkward items such as a pushchair, wheelchairs, golf clubs or surf board, since you may be charged extra or might not be allowed to bring them into the cabin.

Be aware of increased international security requirements, and remove any folding pocket knives or other sharp objects from carry-on baggage. When in doubt, check with your airline.

CHECK-IN, PASSPORT CONTROL, & CUSTOMS

- Plan to arrive at the airport a full two-and-a-half hours before your scheduled departure time for check-in. Have tickets and passport readily accessible.

- Find your flight number on the TV monitors located at airport entrances to find your check-in desk. You will receive your boarding pass and your luggage will be checked. ❶ It is very important that you keep your luggage receipts – you will not be allowed to leave the airport in the Dominican Republic with your luggage without these as proof of ownership.
- Find your designated departure gate. Boarding will begin about thirty minutes before flight time. Those travelling with small children or the elderly should listen for the first boarding call, which gives these groups special preference.

During your stay

ARRIVAL

Purchasing a Tourist Card Every visitor that comes to the Dominican Republic must first purchase a Tourist Card, which enables the holder to legally stay in the country for 90 days. You will need to get this card before passing through immigration and customs, and it is important that you do not lose it since it is needed in order to leave the country as well. If you lose your card, you will have to pay a fine and buy another one. No matter what country you are flying in from or where you hold your passport, the Tourist Card (at the time of writing) must be paid for with $10 in US currency; keep in mind that upon departure there will be an exit tax of $20 US. If you want to stay longer than 90 days, you are required to get an extension. There is an office on the Malecón in Santo Domingo at Centro de Los Heroes (☎ 809 534 8060) that processes requests quickly. Fines for overstays can be as high as RD$200.

Embarkation/disembarkation cards You will have filled these out during your flight or passage and will need to have them ready to present to immigration officers, along with your Tourist Card and other documentation.

Immigration & customs When approaching immigration, have your passport, Tourist Card and embarkation/disembarkation card ready. After you collect your luggage, it needs to be checked through customs.

Export restrictions and limits

Be sure to check with your own country's import restrictions and limits as well, especially if you are planning on bringing home a large number of cigars or a quantity of alcohol. The following are restricted:

- anything over 100 years old without an Official Export Certificate
- mahogany products
- tortoise shell
- unpolished amber (raw amber).

CONSULATE

UK Consulate ⓐ Avenida 27 de Febrero 233 at Avenida Máximo Gómez, Santo Domingo ⓣ 809 472 7111

COMMUNICATION

Telephones

If you need to call from a payphone, it is easiest to purchase a Communicard, available in stores nearly everywhere. Dial 611 for instructions in English, and dial 1411 for directory information.

You may also wish to check with your mobile phone provider about global roaming options, since there is adequate mobile phone service in the country. If you have a mobile phone that is not in use or would like to buy one there, prepaid cards may be purchased and activated once you arrive.

Internet access

The growing popularity and demand for Internet access has resulted in several options for the traveller looking to get connected:

In-room service Top-of-the-line hotels and resorts now offer free Internet access, while others may charge per minute or hour.

All-inclusive resort Internet cafés The most expensive, but the least susceptible to blackouts, thanks to generator backup. Surf the net, burn CDs, print or send digital photos, all without leaving beachside.

Internet cafés Rates are by the hour and quite inexpensive; services vary but usually include broadband connection and webcams.

CURRENCY

The peso is the Dominican monetary unit. It is designated by the symbol RD$, and comes in coins of 1 and 5 pesos or bills of 10, 20, 50, 100, 500, and 1000. The US Dollar is also traded regularly and many prices at major attractions are listed in this denomination, although pesos are accepted at the current rate of exchange.

Banks Available to cash travellers cheques, although the accessibility and safety of credit and debit cards has made them virtually obsolete. 'Casa de cambios' and ATMs will give equally fair exchange rates. Bank hours are usually Mon–Fri 08.00–16.00 and Sat 09.00–13.00.

Credit cards Accepted at larger stores and hotels, and may be used at any of the ATMs found across the country. If you are depending on your credit card to make purchases, keep in mind that most retailers add a surcharge of up to 16% for the service. You will most likely forfeit your right to haggle for prices, as well.

Cash machines Found nearly everywhere in populated and tourist areas, an equally secure way to receive a fair exchange rate. Some may have no access fee for cash advances; check with your bank before leaving home to learn what affiliation to use to avoid a hefty charge.

ELECTRICITY

The Dominican Republic uses the 110 to 125 volts AC, 60 Hz, flat-pronged plugs electrical system (the same as is used in Canada and the USA), so you will need to bring a travel adapter plub. These are readily available in

---

MAKING TELEPHONE CALLS

To make calls within the Dominican Republic, you must remember to always dial 1 809 and then the number, even if it is a local call.

When calling the UK, dial 011 followed by your country code (UK=44) and the phone number.

In case of emergency dial 911. The police respond rapidly to calls from tourists.

the UK at electrical shops or major chemists. Power cuts are a very common occurrence, and it is a good idea to pack at least one flashlight with fresh batteries. Large hotels and many shops have backup generators.

FACILITIES FOR VISITORS WITH DISABILITIES

With so many choices of brand-new, all-inclusive resorts designed for tourists with every type of need, visitors with disabilities should have a much easier time getting the most out of their stay than just a decade or two ago. Most public facilities and museums in the country are unfortunately not set up for wheelchairs, and you will find that streets, shops, and restaurants in towns and cities will often be equally frustrating.

GETTING AROUND

Car hire & driving Major international car rental companies and several locally owned outfits have offices located directly at each major airport. A valid driver's licence from your country of origin is sufficient to be allowed to operate a vehicle here.

Driving tips

- Always keep your petrol tank at least half full – petrol stations close very early and often run out of fuel (purchase it when you can).
- Become acquainted with your spare tyre (and be sure your car is supplied with this and a car-jack) – punctured tyres are common.
- When driving through a large puddle after rainstorms, do not take your foot off the gas entirely. Keep enough exhaust flowing out of the tailpipe to prevent water from entering, thus deterring a stall.
- Do not simply trust a road map; ask your host and then a local whom you can understand well – often maps are misleading and will bring you onto trails, not roads.

Motoconchos These various two-wheeled vehicles, offered for hire, are an extremely cheap but equally dangerous way to get around; multitudes of tourists are injured and killed riding on them each year.
Buses These are an efficient and inexpensive way to get around. You can

choose between the *primera* bus with air conditioning and toilets to take you on longer trips, or a *gua-gua* for short trips around town to save on taxi fares, depending on your destination and needs. The latter is slow and usually crowded, since it makes many stops and is the main method of transportation for locals. Larger cities offer one step up from that, with limited stops and air conditioning. Bus schedules can be found at all major tourist offices. Even first-class bus rides are inexpensive.

Taxis Cabs usually wait at hotels or other taxi parks such as the airport. If you are in need of a taxi or anticipate needing one, have the phone number handy to call the service. Always ask the price ahead of time and have the exact change ready.

HEALTH & HYGIENE

Health hazards Your exposure to any potential infectious disease will depend greatly on your activities during your stay. Those who plan to stay within the perimetres of an all-inclusive resort will likely not need to take as many precautions as travellers bound for a week-long hike up Pico Duarte, but one's own physical condition should also be taken into consideration. Discuss the issue thoroughly with your doctor if there are any concerns. The most common vaccinations recommended for those visiting are hepatitis A and typhoid, although they are not required. If you do have these innoculations, it should be at least two weeks before you leave.

Water Water in the Dominican Republic should not be ingested, even to brush your teeth. Unless you are staying at a very high-end resort hotel, use bottled water for anything that touches your mouth. This is especially true for those who are elderly or ill or otherwise susceptible to infection. It is very important, however, to drink plenty of fluids, including water, during your stay, especially when the temperatures are high, since dehydration can be a problem. The hot climate, change in diet, and often increased alcohol consumption that accompany many holidays encourage this condition, and it is wise to head it off early with several bottles of water each day to prevent symptoms such as dizziness, headaches, muscle cramps, and dark urine.

OPENING HOURS

Shops and boutiques typically open at 08.30 and close for siesta between noon and 14.00, reopening until 18.30. In heavily populated and tourist areas, you may find extended store hours and perhaps even stores open during siesta to meet tourist demands. Most restaurants in any resort region open by 10.00 and will not close until at least 22.00, most likely later, and are open daily, unless family operated. Museums and tour companies also tend to keep open throughout the day, typically open from 09.00 to 18.00 and may be closed on Mondays.

POST

If you want your postcards to arrive home before you do, and within a month, you will have to post them special delivery – and even that does not guarantee anything.

TIME

The Dominican Republic maintains Eastern Standard Time, which is five hours behind GMT.

TIPPING

As a result of terribly low wages, tipping is very important to those employed in the service and tourism industry, especially at entry-level positions. In some jobs, as in other countries, it is expected that tips will be received and therefore little or no salary is paid. As long as service was acceptable, it is customary to tip waiters, porters, housekeepers and tour guides:

- Leaving 10% to 15% of the total restaurant bill is average for waiters.
- Leave your tips in cash when paying by credit card to ensure your server receives it.
- Consider using $US – one dollar will be more appreciated than its equivalent in pesos.
- Housekeepers receive about $1–$2 US per night; it is best to leave this in an envelope marked 'gracias' on the bureau each morning (envelopes for this purpose can be acquired from the hotel desk).

THE LANGUAGE

Dominicans do their best to cater to the needs of English-speaking visitors, but it is considered polite, and sometimes necessary, to know simple phrases in Spanish to show respect and make your travels easier.

ENGLISH
General vocabulary

SPANISH (pronunciation)

yes	*sí* (see)
no	*no* (noh)
thank you	*gracias* (GRAH-see-ahs)
hello	*hola* (OH-la)
goodbye	*adiós* (AW-dee-ohs)
good morning	*buenos días* (BWHE-nos DEE-ahs)
good afternoon	*buenos tardes* (BWHE-nos TAR-dehs)
good evening/night	*buenos noches* (BWHE-nos NO-chays)
I'm sorry	*lo siento* (loh see-EN-toh)
please	*por favor* (pohr fah-BOHR)
excuse me	*perdón* (pehr-dohn) or *permiso* (pehr-MEE-soh)
you're welcome	*de nada* (de NAda)
Help!	*Socorro* (So-KO-ro)
How much is it?	*Cuanto cuesta* (KWAN-toh KWES-tah)
What time is it?	*Que hora es?* (Kay O-ra Ess)
toilets	*los baños* (lohs BAHN-Yohs)
gentlemen	*hombres* (OHM-brays)
ladies	*señoritas* (seen-yohr-EET-ahs)
open	*abierto* (ahb-YARE-toh)
closed	*cerrado* (sahr-ODD-oh)
beach	*playa* (PLY-uh)
church	*iglesia* (ee-GLAY-see-uh)
museum	*museo* (moo-SAY-oh)
I am looking for the...	*Estoy buscando...* (Ess-TOY boos-KAHN-doh)
Do you speak English?	*Habla usted inglés?* (Ablah OOsted eenGLES)
I don't understand	*No comprendo* (No com-PREN-doh)
I understand	*Comprendo* (Com-PREN-doh)

ENGLISH	SPANISH (pronunciation)

General vocabulary (continued)

the bus	*el autobu`s* (el ow-tow-BOOS)
the airplane	*el avión* (el ah-vee-ON)
airport	*aeropuerto* (ay-roh-PWAYR-toh)
the ship	*el barco* (el BAR-ko)
ticket office	*boletería* (bow-lay-tahr-EE-ah)

Health & safety matters

I'm allergic to ...	*Soy alergico(a*) a...* (Soy ah-LAYR-gee-koh ah)
...nuts	*...las fruta secas* (lahs FROO-tahs SAY-kas)
...antibiotics	*....los antibióticos* (lows ahn-tee-by-OH-tee-kohs)
...penicillin	*...la penicilina* (la pe-nee-see-LEE-nah)
I am...	*Estoy...* (Es-TOY)
...pregnant	*...embarazada* (em-bar-ah-SAH-dah)
...sick	*...enfermo(a)* (ehn-FEHR-moh)
Call an ambulance	*Llame una ambulancia* (YA-may OO-nah ahm-byu-LAHN-see-uh)
doctor	*un médica* (oon MEHD-ee-ka)
police	*la policia* (la po-lee-SEE-uh)
emergency	*emergencia* (eh-mer-KHEN-see-uh)
pharmacy	*la farmacia* (la far-mah-SEE-uh)

Days of the week

Monday	*lunes* (LOO-nays)
Tuesday	*martes* (MAR-tays)
Wednesday	*miercoles* (me-HER-ko-les)
Thursday	*jueves* (who-EV-ehs)
Friday	*viernes* (vee-AYR-nays)
Saturday	*sabado* (SAH-baa-doh)
Sunday	*domingo* (doh-MIN-goh)

ACKNOWLEDGEMENTS

We would like to thank all the photographers, picture libraries and organisations for the loan of the photographs reproduced in this book, to whom copyright in the photograph belongs:
AM Corporation/Alamy (page 41); Catherine Karnow/CORBIS (page 71); Franz-Marc Frei/Corbis (page 81); Getty Images (page 29); Giraude Phillipe/Corbis Sygma (page 44); JupiterImages Corporation (pages 93, 111, 125); Layne Kennedy/Corbis (page 88); Ludovic Maisant/Corbis (page 83); Orlando Barria/epa/Corbis (page 109); PCL/Alamy (page 25); Stephen Frink Collection/Alamy (page 26); Terry Harris/Alamy (page 31); Thomas Cook Tour Operations Ltd (pages 1, 5, 9, 10, 13, 36, 50, 57, 61, 62, 65, 75, 95, 98, 103, 105, 107); Tom Bean/Corbis (pages 73, 79); Tony Arruza/Corbis (page 32); Wilmar Photography.com/Alamy (pages 66, 68).

We would also like to thank the following for their contribution to this series: John Woodcock (map and symbols artwork); Katie Greenwood (picture research); Patricia Baker, Rachel Carter, Judith Chamberlain-Webber, Nicky Falkof, Nicky Gyopari, Robin Pridy (editorial support); Christine Engert. Suzie Johanson, Jane Prior, Barbara Theisen (design support).

Send your thoughts to
books@thomascook.com

- Found a beach bar, peaceful stretch of sand or must-see sight that we don't feature?

- Like to tip us off about any information that needs a little updating?

- Want to tell us what you love about this handy, little guidebook and more importantly how we can make it even handier?

Then here's your chance to tell all! Send us ideas, discoveries and recommendations today and then look out for your valuable input in the next edition of this title. And, as an extra 'thank you' from Thomas Cook Publishing, you'll be automatically entered into our exciting monthly prize draw.

Send an email to the above address or write to:
HotSpots Project Editor, Thomas Cook Publishing, PO Box 227, Unit 15/16, Coningsby Road, Peterborough PE3 8SB, UK.